LOVING

Like a Leader

Featuring
77 More Leadership Mints

By PETER JEFF

C omprised of 77 short stories called *Leadership Mints*, **LOVING Like a Leader** is a handy reference tool that demonstrates how love in a business context can spark greater productivity, profitability and sustainability. These *Leadership Mints*, sweetened with insights from 77-plus other books on leadership, illustrate the bottom-line impact of emotional intelligence in general and empathy in particular. And like a candy mint, these *Leadership Mints* are quickly accessed, easily digested and immediately reinvigorating.

LEADERSHIP MINTS PUBLISHING
Grand Rapids, Michigan

A Leadership Mints Series Book

ISBN- 978-069-262-0007 Revised 9-1-17

© 2017, Peter Jeff

The
Leadership Mints
Series

LOVING Like a Leader, *Featuring 77 More Leadership Mints,* is the second book in the Leadership Mints Series designed to help busy leaders refresh and rejuvenate their servant leadership skills. Consumed like a breath mint —quick and on-the-go—a LEADERSHIP MINT is a short story that energizes leadership behaviors and personalizes leadership principles so they are more easily remembered, more readily acted upon and more fully applied. Like its candy counterpart, a LEADERSHIP MINT is easily spooned, quickly digested and immediately reinvigorating.

The first book in the Leadership Mints Series introduced the concept of the 5-Minute Leadership Mints Break that could be conducted as part of on-going staff meetings to provide professional development opportunities in a time-sensitive convenient program. That book —*Leadership Mints, 101 Bite-sized Ideas to Energize Yourself & Others,* was updated, revised and relaunched in 2016 under a new title that better focused on what readers appreciated most about the book: energizing them to take action in 16 different leadership principles. The new title: **THINKING Like a Leader**, *Featuring 101 Leadership Mints.* The intent of that first book in the Leadership Mints Series was to provide busy leaders a tool to fire themselves and others up. The intent of this second book in the Leadership Mints Series — **LOVING Like a Leader** —is to help busy leaders keep from burning themselves and others out.

Other books By Peter Jeff in this
Leadership Mints Series:

THINKING
Like a Leader
Featuring
101 Leadership Mints

BEHAVING
Like a Loving Leader

How do loving leaders behave in quest of bottom-line effectiveness? Consider these key tenets:*

- Achieve results from setting and measuring goals that inspire passion, optimism and purpose.
- Coach for continuous improvement in meeting and exceeding goals.
- Proactively engage in the personal growth of others to achieve their potential.
- Recognize and celebrate the greatness in others.
- Cultivate fulfilling relationships with your personal communications skills. Admit your mistakes. Apologize in person.
- Facilitate meaningful group interactions that engender trust.
- Foster a team community committed to each other and the pursuit of a common goal.

* Adapted from *Everybody Matters*, a leadership development book by Bob Chapman and Raj Sisodia. These tenets stem from a Leadership Checklist inspired by Chapman, Chief Executive Officer of Barry-Wehmiller Companies and utilized by 11,000 employees at this $2.5 billion manufacturing technology and consulting company headquartered in St. Louis, MO.

Refreshing Your

EMPATHY

With Leadership Mints

E mpathy is good business. You gain greater buy-in the more you can step into the shoes of your customers or your employees and more readily feel what they feel. That empathy then fuels a trust that triggers greater productivity and profitability over time. But how do you teach empathy? You don't.

Let others do it for you in this book: like Generals in the U.S. Army (Colin Powell and Norm Schwarzkopf), political leaders like Abraham Lincoln, Harry Truman, Barack Obama and Lee Kuan Yew along with legendary sports heroes like pro football's Vince Lombardi and professional golf's Jack Nicklaus. And here's the best part:

It takes just 5 minutes. Five minutes is the average reading time for each of the 77 short stories (called *Leadership Mints*) personalizing 18 specific leadership behaviors. That's what this book **LOVING Like a Leader** is all about: winning with feeling.

CONTENTS

(See Table of Contents page 241 for list
of all *77 Leadership Mints*)

Quick Peek Inside

Turn to page 232 for the **Behavioral Index**, a listing of each of the *77 Leadership Mints* (stories) organized alphabetically according to 18 leadership behaviors from Adapting to Vulnerability. Other key navigational tools in the book include:

Today's EngageMINT

To help you better define and apply the key leadership learning, each of the 77 Leadership Mints begins with a one-line summary called an EngageMINT. It is formatted like this with an icon shaped like a mint.

1. See a list of all 77 **EngageMINTS** beginning on page 237.

2. See the **Overview** (page 234) of the *77 Leadership Mints* by category (Compassion, Connection and Conviction).

3. See the **Epilogue** (page 199) to assess the business rationale for leading with love.

4. See the **Afterword** (page 211) for initiatives you could use to become an even more effective loving leader.

5. See the **Appendix** (page 219) for tips on honing your sense of humor to become a more effective loving leader.

6. See ***Cashing In On Love*** page 200.

"If you can't love
quit trying
to be a leader."

Former CEO Gerry Czarnecki,
writing in his book *Lead With Love.*

Refreshing Your Empathy
With Leadership Mints

Protesters marching through the streets. Gridlock in Congress. Millions of Dilbert-dazed office workers staggering like Zombies through the cubicle-crazed corporate graveyard from 9 a.m. to 5 p.m. And millions more of device-carrying, screen-staring, thumb-texting employees— so mesmerized they care more about what others like themselves feel or think on Facebook or Twitter—to care much about anything or anyone else. Especially on the job. Whoa there, Bad News Breath! Isn't there anything a leader can do to turn the enraged into the engaged? Sure. But shhhh! It's a secret.

It's such a power-packed secret that if a leader applies it knowingly and carefully it has the potential to stir interest, foster creativity, build teamwork, engender trust, instill confidence, reinforce credibility, spark innovation, increase productivity and strengthen profitability. It's a secret that can ameliorate the isolation and polarization of our politics and stimulate meaning into our working lives. It's a secret born in our need as human beings to be appreciated and bred in our relationships to be validated. And the secret is (wait for it) love.

Who says that love is the best-kept secret of successful leaders? Researchers James Kouzes and Barry Posner and they should know after assessing and interviewing over two million corporate and non-profit leaders all over the world in the last 30 years. As the authors of *The Leadership Challenge*—the most-sold leadership development book with over 1.5 million copies—Kouzes and Posner state emphatically that not only is "love the best-kept secret of successful leaders" but also that: "Of all the things that sustain a leader over time, love is the most lasting." Building on the research of Kouzes and Posner, **LOVING Like a Leader** comprises 77 short stories called <u>Leadership Mints</u>. These stories illustrate how a caring and sharing mindset (love in a business context) can engage others to be more productive, more collaborative and more innovative. That's a challenge these days when more than 7 in 10 of your employees are disengaged according to Gallup. The vast majority of your employees don't care about their job or your customers because they think in part their leaders don't care about them. That's why this book is designed as a refresher for sharing and caring leaders and as a catalyst for those leaders who have lost that loving feeling in the wake of so much corporate malaise, political gamesmanship and social unrest. The first step in parlaying your power as a loving leader is to strengthen and sharpen your sense of empathy—your ability to participate with others in their ideas and feelings.

Empathy is Counter-Intuitive

Yet for many leaders, "empathy is counter-intuitive," according to research conducted by the Franklin Covey Company. After assessing hundreds of thousands of leaders, the leadership development firm found that empathy is the least practiced leadership skill. Other research confirms the lack of a feel for feelings that negatively impacts the bottom line. For example, engaging people is the top weakness of Chief Executive Officers, according to Stanford University's Center for Leadership Development & Research. And the Conference Board calls recruiting and retaining human capital the top challenge facing business leaders. That's why these *Leadership Mints*—these 77 short stories in this book—are designed to stimulate your loving feeling (empathy) with examples from business, politics and sports.

Like a candy mint, these *Leadership Mints* are easily accessed, immediately satisfying and quickly digested in 5 minutes, the average reading time of each Mint. You don't have to sit down to read this book for 15-30 minutes or more at a time as if it were a meal to gain some insight you can use on the job. You can grab 'n go. You can digest a *Leadership Mint* on the go as if it were a candy mint. Consider this book your personal candy mint dish to grab 'n go when a leader's intervention can do the most good: in real time, solving a real issue relevant to all concerned at the time. This dish of *Leadership Mints*, packaged in a reader-friendly format of short stories and packing vital leadership thinking, provides a quick and easy solution to the long-term growth and development of current and future leaders without sacrificing short term productivity to attend an off-site seminar or workshop. That's the intent of a *Leadership Mint,* a quick pick-me-up via a short entertaining 5-minute story that provides a key tip or technique to handle a leadership issue ranging from conflict management to emotional intelligence.

Sweetened with insights from 77-plus other books on leadership, these 77 *Leadership Mints*—short stories personalizing leadership principles—demonstrate how loving leaders leverage their bottom-line by keeping their people top of mind and treating their employees and customers with even more dignity and respect. The 77 *Leadership Mints* are segmented into three categories: Compassion, Connection and Conviction. Each category is intended to help the reader/leader define and develop their own understanding and application of love as a leadership behavior rooted in a solid business rationale. See the **Epilogue** on page 199 for the business case for leading with love. See the **Behavioral Index** (page 232) for a listing of each of the 77 *Leadership Mints* (stories) organized alphabetically according to 18 leadership behaviors from Adapting to Vulnerability. And see the **Appendix** (page 219) for a 10-page section on tips to enhance your sense of humor—the essence of love—according to historian Thomas Carlyle.

Savor these 77 *Leadership Mints* that spotlight key behaviors of loving leaders including an optimistic coaching and coaxing mindset, constructive feedback delivered with dignity and respect and affirmation of their employees first and foremost as human beings with personal interests, needs and concerns that must FIRST be addressed. However before embarking on this concept of leading with love, let's have lunch: Chinese.

Remember the first time you used a pair of chopsticks? Chances are you ended up with a splattering of sweet and sour sauce on your shirt or blouse. No wonder. You were trying to "manage" that morsel of Hunan chicken into your mouth. Later you learned how to use both chopsticks at the same time to manage AND lead simultaneously to get the food into your mouth with no splatter. Mastering chopsticks demands both stability (management) AND flexibility (leadership) at the same time as you can see in the following basic steps to eating with chopsticks: Hold the lower chopstick firmly against your middle finger. Hold the upper chopstick as you would hold a pencil. Keep the lower chopstick steady (manage for stability) while moving the upper chopstick up and down (lead with flexibility). That dichotomy—one chopstick stationary and the other chopstick moving—takes some getting used to. So does managing and leading at the same time.

You need both skill sets to be effective in either discipline. You need stability—planning, budgeting, organizing and controlling or management. And you also need flexibility—values, vision, creativity, caring, sharing, framing and strategic positioning or leading. That's why the most effective loving leaders brandish both stability and flexibility as if they're playing chopsticks on the piano with both hands. They demonstrate a broader attitude more than simply a bolder aptitude. Their broader attitude of inclusion and social awareness hones their compassion, connection and conviction.

That's why the most effective loving leaders lead with a love—a COMPASSION—that feeds and feeds off of the feelings of others, feelings that resonate deep inside their souls. They lead with a love—a CONNECTION—that stimulates more listening and learning for enhanced performance and sparks more nurturing and encouraging for increased results. And they lead with a love— a CONVICTION—that spawns more humility and vulnerability and demands more introspection than inspection., knowing that:

_*"The best kept secret*
*of successful leaders is love."**

*James Kouzes and Barry Posner,
writing in their iconic book *The Leadership Challenge*.

PART I

COMPASSION

Beyond the
NUMBers

*E*mpathy is not embedded in a
financial model or a balance
sheet. Yet business schools
have not yet done enough to
wed this reality into their curricula,
to place not just ethics but empathy
alongside corporate finance and
accounting.

**Kim Gittleson, Journalist
and MBA graduate**

Mint 1

Energizing Others
With Empathy

●

Today's EngageMINT

Unlock the treasure buried in the hearts
of your employees.

K nown for his quick temper and defiant ruthlessness, Green Bay Packers Coach Vince Lombardi surprised and even shocked some of his pro football players when he opened a team meeting with a question that immediately silenced the room: "What is the meaning of love?" How absurd from the football coach who said you need to hate in order to win; the same football coach who dismissed pain in his injured players and consistently stoked the fires of hatred and anger on the practice field. "There were times when a lot of those guys would say 'I hate this sonofabitch,'" recalled Max McGee, the former wide receiver.

What's the meaning of love? The question seemed so incongruent, so out of bounds especially in this venue with this particular audience—so called "madmen"— as Lombardi characterized pro football players. But the coach had much more than romance in mind when he broached the 4-letter word that widened the eyes and dropped the jaws of the most jaundiced players that morning. He had winning in mind as cited by David Maraniss in his biography of Lombardi titled *When Pride Still Mattered.* Lombardi's winning-is-everything mantra (actually his <u>will-to</u>-win-is-everything mantra as he later tried to clarify) may have been rooted in that love talk he led that morning.

Lombardi noted that anyone can love someone's good looks or great personality but it takes a real leader to love someone just as much because of who they are — the good, the bad and the ugly. Coach Lombardi coaxed his players to develop a bond with teammates who may not be perfect. That bond, a commitment to caring with a greater sense of empathy, would encourage the less than perfect players to find the best in themselves and then of course their enhanced individual performance would strengthen the team's overall performance. "I don't necessarily have to like my players and associates but as the leader I must love them," Lombardi admitted. His personal example of caring deep down for his players even after his rants soon spread throughout the team and their performance improved dramatically. Here's one example of how Lombardi energized his team with empathy.

The Packers were flying home after losing a Thanksgiving Day football game. The team was hurting: their bodies battered and their egos bruised after losing three out of their first four games that season. And Lombardi seemed to feel their pain as they boarded their chartered plane to lick their wounds. Lombardi reminded himself of that talk he once gave his team on the meaning of love: to help less than perfect players find the best in themselves and others. And then Lombardi walked his talk. He comforted them. And he celebrated their allegiance together. He lifted the ban on beer on the team plane. Then he invited each of his players and their families to a Thanksgiving Day turkey dinner later that evening in Green Bay.

All of that loving paid off. Lombardi's team—feeling appreciated (read loved)—played their hearts out the remaining weeks of the season. That fall the Packers completed their second straight winning season under Lombardi and earned a berth in the NFL Championship Game (the precursor to the Super Bowl). His Packers would go on to win three more NFL Championships including the first two Super Bowls.

But more significantly each member of the team won something much greater. They personally experienced and better understood the answer to Lombardi's question: "What is the meaning of love?" The answer: The opportunity to energize yourself and others with empathy, with shared feelings of caring and sharing. And in "making love," the most effective leaders awaken dormant potential and uncover hidden value in themselves and others to improve performance and bolster the bottom line.

Mint 2

Suffering Like a Leader:
FOR OTHERS

●

Today's EngageMINT

*Beware of walling yourself
off from others.*

Raw emotion choked his voice and gripped his quivering lips as the leader cried on national television. He blamed himself for dashing the hopes of millions counting on him. But he quickly bounced back, demonstrating that scorned leaders have a renewed appreciation for the insights that can come from tears spawned in shared conflict and loss. The leader's insight echoed the off-stage chant from the opera *Tales of Hoffmann* by Jacques Offenbach:

> *"One is made great through love.
> One is made greater through tears."*

Lee Kuan Yew, then the Prime Minister of Singapore, teared up and broke down during a news conference on live television in 1965 when Malaysia expelled Singapore, leaving the small island-country to fend for itself. The Prime Minister's five million constituents were counting on him to strengthen their economic ties to Malaysia and therefore their personal security and prosperity. He failed them. He felt so responsible, so distraught, the Prime Minister could hardly speak. At one point, the Prime Minister— biting his lip and fighting back tears—could only respond to a question from a journalist with 49 seconds of heart-felt silence. But then he regained his composure, renewed his commitment to his constituents and rebuilt their nation even stronger than before. Over the next three decades, he led Singapore from a decrepit outpost without its own water supply and no natural resources into becoming a rich and robust world commercial center. And in the process, Lee Kuan Yew 's anguish demonstrated what author Howard Haas opines in his book *The Leader Within*: "Leadership is less about sheer talent than about introspection forged from suffering." Psychologists tell us that suffering can expose deeply hidden vulnerabilities that make a leader more sensitive to new ideas, new perspectives, and new solutions. That's why the most effective leaders find it instructive that the word "compassion" stems from the Latin word that means "to suffer with." And significantly the fact that man is the only animal on earth who cries isn't lost on the most effective leaders. They see their tears as a stimulant that engages their humanity, awakens their dreams and enlivens their lives. They identify with Tom Wingo, the fictional hero in Pat Conroy's novel *The Prince of Tides.* His eyes well up with tears after reading one of his sister's poems. He says: "It was good to feel the tears try to break through. It was proof I was still alive, inside down deep....."

Beyond The NUMBers

Yet, baring those feelings takes courage, the courage to confront your failures head on, the courage to look your constituents in the eye, the courage to look at yourself in the mirror. It's too easy to bury your feelings in a stack of papers on your desk, as author John Steinbeck observed in *Grapes of Wrath.* He said the "owner men worshipped their data as a refuge from thought and from feeling." It's too tempting to numb yourself with all those NUMBers. It's too tempting to think of yourself as if you were a rock or an island because as Simon and Garfunkel sang "a rock feels no pain and an island never cries." But the loving leader in you knows better.

You lead best when your feelings are carefully and thoughtfully released for others not simply emotionally unleashed for yourself— when your feelings are freed from confinement or restraint not simply set loose to pursue at will as the dictionary defines releasing vs. unleashing. And you lead best when you understand and embrace the notion that "compassion is empathy in action," as Ellie Allison Napolitano writes in *Flywheel.* With that empathy in action, loving leaders leverage their feelings as an advent for others not simply a vent for themselves. They don't cry for themselves. They cry out for others. Even on national television.

Mint 3

Crying Like a Leader:
FOR OTHERS

Today's EngageMINT
*Shed your tears
for others not yourself.*

S cared. The four-star general in the United States Army –all 6-foot-3 and 240 pounds of him – was scared. Not on the battlefield. After all he led the US coalition of troops from 30 countries to victory in the Persian Gulf War in 1991. No, General Norman Schwarzkopf was even more scared of unarmed men who couldn't or wouldn't cry. "Frankly, any man who doesn't cry scares me a little bit," Schwarzkopf admitted to Barbara Walters on ABC television's 20/20 program in March 1991. "I don't think I would like a man who was incapable of enough emotion to get tears in his eyes every now and then. That person scares me; he's not a human being."

Leaders are first and foremost human beings. Not turn-around artists. Not merger & acquisition gurus. Not generals. Not presidents. Not popes. They are first and foremost human beings. They cry. The first US Army General to win a major war in 46 years, Schwarzkopf noted that General Ulysses S. Grant cried when he learned of President Abraham Lincoln's death. General Dwight Eisenhower wiped away tears when he saw the planes take off on the eve of D-day knowing he could be sending most of those pilots to their deaths. And President Lincoln wept when he visited the injured soldiers during the Civil War. Even legendary football coach Vince Lombardi would cry when giving an emotional speech to his Green Bay Packers. Confident leaders know their "tears are a great gift from God—a safety-valve built into our system," notes author Alan Loy McGinnis in his book *The Friendship Factor*. That's why leaders realize that crying (expressing their humanity) and relationship building (connecting to the feelings and concerns of others) anchor the behaviors of strong, determined and competitive leaders. In fact, a study reported in the *Journal of Psychology of Men & Masculinity* found that football players who cried had higher levels of self-esteem which gave them a competitive edge on and off the field. Real men (and women) cry—FOR others. They feel what others are feeling as they meld into an organic whole of shared feelings. In fact the most authentic criers first "see their own tears in the other person's eyes" observes Reverend Forrest Church in his book *Life Craft: The Art of Meaning in the Everyday.*

The tears of a loving leader are shed for what is significant to others —what's pithy—not what's a pity. No leader ever throws a Pity Party. They're too busy turning the spotlight on their followers. They're too busy streaming their tears and the tears of their followers into a river of mutual caring and comfort filled with currents of a collective trust in the present and hope for the future. They're too busy focused on letting down their personal guard so their followers can get so close to their leaders that the followers can see themselves in the leader's eyes and the leader can see himself or herself in the eyes of their followers.

Consider how Barack Obama saw himself in the eyes of others the morning after winning re-election as President of the United States of America in 2012. The President teared up thanking his volunteers and staff at his Chicago campaign headquarters. He was being real. A study at Pennsylvania State University said tears in a man are a sign of honesty. And in being honest with himself and even more real to others the President focused on their feelings more than on his own. There were no national television cameras in that room. This was to be a more personal, more intimate, kick-off your shoes moment of triumph that he clearly earned. Yet Obama, wiping away a tear and choking up, quickly turned the spotlight on his followers: "I'm really proud of all of you. The most important thing you need to know is that your journey's just beginning," Obama said, his sense of empathy resonating with a keen personal insight to feel what they were feeling deep in their souls. Perhaps someday one of them may even become a president or a four-star general who cries. Like a leader. For others. Intentionally.

Mint 4

Kissing Like a Leader:
FOR OTHERS

●

Today's EngageMINT
Appreciate others with intentional listening.

Pucker up. How good a kisser are you? Your kissing behavior could be a measure of your leadership capability. What? Non-sense you say. Well consider the following description of an optimal kiss in this excerpt from Robert A. Heinlein's novel: *Stranger in a Strange Land:*

"Anne tell me something. What's so special about the way Michael kisses?" Anne looked dreamy and then dimpled. "Michael gives a kiss his whole attention."

"Oh, rats! I do too." Anne shook her head.
"No, some men try to. Men who did a very good job of it indeed have kissed me. But they don't really give kissing a woman their whole attention. They can't. No matter how hard they try, some parts of their minds are on something else: Missing the last bus. Their own techniques in kissing. Worry about their jobs. Or money. Or something. Now Michael doesn't have any technique. "But when he kisses you he isn't doing anything else. Not anything. You're his whole universe for that moment. And the moment is eternal because he doesn't have any plans and he isn't going anywhere. Just kissing you." She shivered. "A woman notices. It's overwhelming."

Leaders are great kissers. Loving leaders kiss you with something more overwhelming, more engaging and more exciting than their lips. They kiss you with their full and complete attention. They kiss you with their eyes. They kiss you with their ears. They kiss you with a magnetic smile that bathes you in a feeling of fidelity and security, in a feeling of warmth and understanding, and in a feeling of complete acceptance and validation. They kiss you with empathy, with feeling what you are feeling in the moment. And they kiss you with a feeling of reverence, of respect, or high regard.

When you regard someone or something, the dictionary says you show "respect or consideration." You take a "protective interest." You "estimate the worth of something or someone." You become like the sheep rancher in the movie *Babe* when he first visually kisses the pig—Babe. The narrator says that the rancher and the pig did more than just eye each other. "They regarded each other."

Turning a Routine Encounter Into a Memorable Experience

Loving leaders in particular regard each person on their teams sincerely and intimately. Their eyes become your eyes and your sense of empathy deepens into "seeing things through their eyes" as actress Jane Fonda defined intimacy in an interview with Oprah Winfrey. With that sense of intimacy, leaders as great kissers, can turn a routine encounter into a memorable experience. Consider the post office customer who wanted to send a package first class. The post office clerk looked into the eyes of the customer— carefully regarding him—and then planted a verbal kiss on his lips: "I'll mark it first class right here before your eyes," she said.

That loving leader made her customer feel a sense of recognition and appreciation. She regarded him and he felt special at least in that moment. Someone had acknowledged him and truly listened to him. Intently. That's what leaders do. Even in routine transactions, the most effective leaders don't kiss you OFF. They turn you ON. Intentionally. Purposefully. And professionally.

Mint 5

General to the Troops:
"I Shall Always Love You!"
●
Today's EngageMINT
*Love others to bring out
the best in them.*

General Norman Schwarzkopf surprised a lot of battle-worn military leaders when he publicly stated to his troops and colleagues: "I shall always love you! I will never, ever, ever forget you." No that isn't a line out of a sexy movie or an excerpt from a sensational tabloid. Significantly, those words gushed from the heart of a four-star General in the United States Army during a speech he delivered to his fellow military leaders and a national television audience. The General pledged his love to the soldiers he led to victory in the Persian Gulf War in 1991. Schwarzkopf was retiring from the army after 31 years. But he said he could never retire from his soldiers. He was confident and not the least guarded or embarrassed in expressing his most sincere and genuine feeling that caring leaders and committed followers (employees) are lovers who sustain each other's high standards of performance. The more they worked together, the more they cared for each other, the more they looked out for each other, the more they enhanced their collective and individual performance.

Retired Marine General James Mattis, appointed Secretary of Defense in 2017, agrees. Mattis says "that kind of affection brings out self-discipline where people don't want to let down their unit and will keep fighting even to their peril." *(See related research page 204.)* To foster and sustain that affection among the troops, Mattis notes that leaders must earn the trust of their troops every single day with their actions, with caring for and sharing with their troops, with listening and learning from them, with seeking to know them personally–at least on a human level. That's why four months before D-Day, General Dwight Eisenhower visited troops in 26 divisions at 24 air fields and on five warships. The leader of the Allied Forces would chat with individual troops on where they were from often asking about the fishing prospects there. In essence Eisenhower felt compelled to express up close his appreciation for—and love of—the soldier on the front lines. Eisenhower used those visits with the troops to refresh himself as much as boost their morale. "Whenever I became fed up with meetings, paperwork and protocol, I could rehabilitate myself by a visit with the troops talking to each of them as individuals and listening to each other's stories," Eisenhower said. "I was refreshed and could return to headquarters reassured that hidden behind administrative entanglements the military was an enterprise manned by human beings." Human beings. Not troops. Human beings. Not employees. Human beings. Not voters. Human beings. Not stockholders. And those human beings embrace their potential more with a spark from the loving leader.

That's why the former president and chief executive officer of Scandinavian Airlines observed, "You have to manage by love." Jan Carlzon adds: "You have to create an atmosphere in which people feel they are respected, that you have faith in them, even that you love them. Then they will dare to take risks. Dare to use their imagination." And then with love leaders become even more committed, even more focused, even more authentic as Susan Scott notes in her book *Fierce Conversations*: "Authenticity is a powerful attraction. When we free our true selves and release the energy others recognize it and respond. It is as if we have set ourselves ablaze. Others are attracted to the warmth and add their logs to the fire." And they fire up the performance of others.

Take it from Reggie Jackson, the prolific home run hitter of Mr. October fame. He felt the warmth of an authentic leader–a loving leader –and blazed his way into the Baseball Hall of Fame over a 21-year career. "A great manager has a knack for making ballplayers think they are better than they think they are," Jackson said. "He forces you to have a good opinion of yourself. He lets you know he believes in you. He makes you get more out of yourself. And once you learn how good you really are, you never settle for playing anything less than your very best."

Mint 6

Declaring Your Interdependence

●

Today's EngageMINT
Relying on others
fortifies your leadership.

Honk! Honk! Honk! Flying together, the flock of geese honk at each other to keep themselves in a more efficient formation with each encouraging the other, each feeding off the other and each even becoming the other at times where the leader becomes the follower and the follower becomes the leader. Flying interdependently in formation, these geese demonstrate the symbiotic relationship between a loving leader and his or her followers (employees). They need each other to perform at their best just as every bow needs its arrow, every bell needs its clapper and every pen needs its ink. Together they bring out the best in each other. They work with each other not for one another. They invest in each other. They trust each other. They rely on each other. They turn their collective energy into a synergy that generates greater productivity—much like the 71% farther that geese fly in formation according to researchers. And together the leader and the follower—assuming each other's responsibilities at times—become more productively engaged, more creatively enriched and more personally fulfilled as poet Mary Carolyn Davis observes in: *This is Friendship:*

> *"I love you, not only for what you*
> *are, but for what I am with you. I love you*
> *not for what you have made of yourself,*
> *but for what you are making of me."*

Okay, maybe love is too strong a word for the relationship between the leader and his or her followers. Or is it? (See page 201 *Defining Love in a Business Context*). At any rate, that sense of interdependence makes for a long-lasting and fruitful relationship. That sense of interdependence becomes like an umbilical cord especially for newly promoted leaders who need to stay connected more than ever before against the odds. However newly promoted executives "spend less time in meaningful interaction with their staff and lose sight of how their emotional states impact those around them," according to Forbes magazine's Travis Bradberry.

Sharing The Leadership Spotlight
To Brighten the Performance

The leader who has lost that loving feeling for his or her direct reports rationalizes that there can only be one lead-dog pulling the sled. And that's the leader with all the pull: the leader whose name is on the door. Not so fast says Richard Branson, the founder of the most billion dollar companies in the most industry segments. "It is the job of the lead dog to go out of his way to make sure the rest of the team gets to see the bigger picture," says Branson. Especially loving leaders. They realize that the more they share the burden and the spotlight, the more REAL pull the leader has whose name is on the door.

That's why the most effective leaders create more engagement opportunities with and for their staffs. They figuratively fly in formation with their staffs. They see the world from their employee's vantage point. And they share the lead at least temporarily with their direct reports in a spirit of interdependence. They embrace the symbiotic value of a community that needs leaders, heeds followers and feeds off of each other. Together they develop the individuals in the community and bring out the community in the individuals. That's because loving leaders know that "the community stagnates without the impulse of the individual," as author William James observed. "And the impulse dies away without the sympathy of the community." One needs the other for optimum performance.

Mint 7

Standing Outside of Yourself
In Sheer Ecstasy

●

Today's EngageMINT
*Step outside of yourself
to gain insight into others.*

cstasy. Imagine feeling sheer ecstasy! Fully clothed. On the job. Every day. Drug free. Yes, you read that correctly: Ecstasy. And no, you are not reading one of those tabloids that have corrupted the term—Ecstasy—to mean a hallucinogenic street drug. Actually, the word —Ecstasy—stems from the Greek 'ex stasis', meaning "to stand outside of yourself." Sober. Clear headed. Distinctively decided. That ability "to stand outside of yourself" may well be the distinctive and differentiating factor of loving leaders in particular and humanity in general as Eric Newton writes in his book The *Arts of Man*: "One of the basic differences between man and the animals is his power to stand outside himself."

Standing outside of yourself is the only way to appreciate others, to discern reality on its terms not yours, to think about your thinking, and to sense and make sense of your emotional intelligence. Exercising that differentiating factor—standing outside yourself—is a key leadership skill that is often buried deep in the arrogance of wanna-be leaders too wrapped up in themselves and their own egos and ideas. Loving leaders know that when you can't or won't step outside of yourself you can't step into a new world of opportunity. Your indifference to the different stagnates your potential.

When you can't step out beyond yourself you have no real sense of comparison. No real basis for perspective. No real understanding of value. That's why the most effective leaders know that without ecstasy, they can become too self-absorbed, too self-righteous, and too all-knowing. The most effective leaders know that they DON'T know. They know they need to let go of their preconceived notions. They need to get lost in something other than themselves. They need to unleash their feelings outside of themselves. In sheer ecstasy.

Loving leaders can step away from their own ego and arrogance long enough to bathe in the glow of another's ideas, notions and opinions and more readily appreciate – "naively and freshly again and again the basic goods of life" as psychologist and author Abraham Maslow wrote in his book *Motivation and Personality.* The most creative and innovative leaders live every day—every hour—as naively and freshly as they can; beyond their own limitations in experience. Step outside of yourself—in sheer ecstasy—to see things from another's perspective. Consider this scenario in a C-Suite meeting.

The architect proudly illustrated his design for a new manufacturing plant. Executives nodded approvingly. Then the CEO stood outside of himself in ecstasy— outside of his position as a fiduciary—and took a step toward serving a greater good.   He noticed that the layout of the manufacturing plant placed the loudest machines adjacent to a residential street. In an instant he made a critical decision to scrap this layout in favor of a new design that inverted the plant layout, placing the other end of the plant (a quieter shipping area) adjacent to the neighbors. "That'll cost us $150,000 to redo this plan," objected the plant manager. But the CEO, in his well-developed, highly-disciplined, value-driven sense of ecstasy, didn't flinch at the financial loss. He said he wanted to "treat those people who live on that street the way I would want to be treated if I lived there."

The CEO's demonstration of his loving leadership –his emotional intelligence–taught his managers a keen leadership lesson that day: Just because you have the right to (fill in the blank) doesn't make it right unless you stand apart from yourself—in sheer ecstasy—and factor in the rights of others.

Mint 8

Keep It Real
You Big Deal

●

Today's EngageMINT
*Be comfortable
in your own skin.*

No matter how high he climbed on the corporate ladder — from the pioneering leader in the film industry to the president of Warner Brothers for more than 20 years — Harry Warner never forgot his roots. In fact, he never figuratively slipped out of his old shoes no matter how well-heeled he had become. The former shoe maker would habitually pick up nails he found walking along the studio's streets and pop them in his mouth just like he did as a boy working in his dad's shoe-repair shop. He knew what all effective leaders come to know: You are what you are no matter where you are. That's why the most effective leaders keep it real, especially when they become a big deal even if they become a global leader of more people than four times the population of the United States or eight times the population of Russia: the pope.

The leader of 1.2 billion Catholics since 2013, Pope Francis earned a populist reputation for his humble lifestyle and his focus on the poor. Some in the media cited his soaring popularity and donned him a rock star. Pope Francis rejected that spotlight saying the pope "is a man who laughs, cries, sleeps calmly and has friends like everyone else." Pope Francis knows that leaders must first connect with themselves—authentically, personally, poignantly— before they can lead others. As author John R. Diekman observes in his book *Human Connections*: "The person who is moving in the direction of effectiveness is tuned into his own self, what he is feeling, what he is thinking and what he is wanting." Socrates taught: Know thyself." Shakespeare wrote: "To thine own self be true." Be comfortable in your own skin. Then and only then can you "establish long-term, meaningful relationships and have the self-discipline to get results," writes Bill George in his book, *Authentic Leadership: Rediscovering the Secrets to Creating Lasting Value.* Then higher performance and increased productivity will follow. At least that's the way one employee describes his leader, his boss (a hotel General Manager) in Jon Katzenbach's book *Peak Performance.* "Robert talks to you as a person not an employee. He treats everyone well not just the senior managers."

That's why loving leaders are incapable of faking concern. Anchored in their personal integrity, they are too grounded in the real world. They shun the pedestal of privilege. They discard the trappings of the rich and famous, no matter how high their rank or how expansive their office or how extensive their financial portfolio. Maybe that's why Peter the Great, the Czar of Russia, assigned himself the lowest rank in the army at age 13 even though he could have made himself commander-in-chief. Peter the Great had the authenticity to earn his rank not command it. He worked with the other troops rather than ruling over them. He kept it real. He toured Europe as a common soldier not as the first Russian Czar to leave his country.

Loving leaders keep it real no matter how much greatness is thrust on them or how many bonus checks they cash. Consider the newly-minted chief executive officer of a two-billion dollar global company. He is fishing through a wad of congratulatory phone messages from industry titans. Unfazed over his instant millionaire status in his first CEO role, he stops shuffling through the phone messages and announces to an aide: "Here's the most important message of them all." The aide reads the phone message: "Your Mom called. She says congratulations." This loving leader would go on to serve nearly two decades as a highly successful CEO who kept his feet firmly on the ground and his head out of the clouds. During his stint in the C-Suite he met many CEOs of large global companies. But he was most impressed with those CEOs who did not seem packaged to play a role. They kept it real. They were comfortable in their own skin. And like him, they never forgot where they came from.

Mint 9

TRANSPARENCY
Even in Your Pajamas

●

Today's EngageMINT
*Be real to close
the deal.*

Wearing only his pajamas and a bathrobe, he stood on the back of a train. In the middle of the night. In the middle of nowhere. He waved to a couple of hundred well-wishers, saying: "I am sorry I had gone to bed. But, I thought you would like to see what I look like. Even if I didn't have on any clothes." Harry S. Truman spoke comfortably and conversationally without notes for 10 minutes on issues the people cared about. Two months later Harry S. Truman was elected President of the United States of America.

Yes, the same self-effacing Harry S. Truman — the one-time farmer and failed businessman; the only U.S. President in the 20th Century who did not graduate from college. Yes, the same Harry S. Truman who grew up a "bespectacled momma's boy," and a "sissy who would always run from fights" according to newspaper accounts. Yes, the same Harry S. Truman who battled the odds as a presidential candidate and defied the pundits. Three weeks before his election, the top 50 reporters covering the presidential race voted AGAINST Truman. But Truman taught all of us a lesson in leadership: Be real. Be transparent. Be authentic. Be believable. And they will follow the leader despite the naysayers.

So how did this plain-spoken Missourian pull off the most famous political upset in U.S. presidential campaign history in 1948 (before Donald Trump stunned the establishment with his political upset victory over Hillary Clinton in 2016)? By being himself. Be real to close the deal. That's the leadership lesson Harry S. Truman taught us in overcoming the odds— personally and professionally. Despite not having any international experience, the first vice president to ascend to the presidency in a time of war successfully ended World War II. With only 83 days in office as vice president before the death of President Franklin Delano Roosevelt, Truman proved presidential in his historic decision-making. He authorized the detonation of the world's first atomic bomb and ended desegregation in the armed forces. Yet, the media of his day said Truman — all 5-feet-8 and 167 pounds—didn't fit the image most people have of the leader of the free world. A reporter said Truman "seemed like a typical small city business man, pleasant and substantial, more at home on Main Street than on Pennsylvania Avenue."

But the media also acknowledged Truman's emotional intelligence, his awareness of himself and his ability to read the emotions of others. One reporter wrote that there was "an agreeable warm-heartedness and simplicity about Truman that is genuine." Another reporter noted that Truman "got down to earth and talked the language of the people." No delusions of self-importance. No strutting in the proverbial Emperor's Clothes. No fancy vanity magazine-like propaganda tools. In fact, Truman distributed a 16-page comic book about his biography and political vision during his presidential campaign. He did not try to obfuscate or pontificate or calculate how to hide behind his title or position. He admitted his vulnerabilities—PUBLICLY—on his first day as President of the United States. In the midst of a world war, he asked reporters, crowding into the Oval Office, to pray for him because he felt "like the moon, the stars and all the planets had fallen on me."

A few weeks later a reporter asked Truman to reflect on his reputation as being an average guy. "Do you think you have made being average more acceptable in society?" Truman rejected the premise of the question and responded: "Well, what's wrong with being average?" Nothing, especially when you are leading BECAUSE OF IT — not in spite of it. Truman's sense of being average helped him better connect with the electorate on their terms—as a loving leader.

Mint 10

AUTHENTICITY
Shine with Less Sheen

Today's EngageMINT
*Vulnerability can be
a source of strength.*

Fishing Tickle. The sign in the bait store window was misspelled. On purpose. Likewise the print ad for the Campbell Soup Company headlined a factual error. On purpose. What's going on here? Incompetence? No, dubitatio. Rhetoricians define dubitatio as doubt or ignorance — feigned or real—used as a rhetorical device to make the speaker/leader seem more human, more real and ultimately more honest.

The most effective leaders double down on their dubitatio. The more vulnerable a leader the more they can reach out and touch the hearts and minds of their followers. Large corporate entities seem more human when they make easily-discovered mistakes in public. Then customers parlay that vulnerability into building a more intimate relationship with that big conglomerate. And sales soar.

That's what happened when The Campbell Soup Company listed 22 different soups in a print ad. But the headline screamed "21 kinds of soup." Lots of customers notified the company of their error. But Campbell Soup, doubling down on its dubitatio, deliberately delayed correcting the error. They figured they would gain more in customer loyalty the longer they demonstrated their vulnerability—especially in an area that had nothing to do with the taste, nutritional value, or safety in the manufacturing process. Leaders know that sometimes you shine with less sheen. Just ask major league baseball pitchers. They never get to pitch a pristine, brand-new baseball right out of the box. Not with the umpires doubling down on their dubitatio. For two hours before every game, the umpires rub all 156 baseballs allocated per game with a specially prepared mud to take the sheen off the ball. Rubbing off that sheen gives the ball a coarser feel that is more readily gripped. The greater the integrity of the grip the more control the pitcher has over the spin and trajectory of the baseball.

That's why the most effective leaders are mindful of rubbing off their sheen. They consistently work at dulling their sheen so others can better see and hear them. Consider the sheen on the tough looking lawyer with the stern military style who could easily intimidate a jury —until he uttered a word or rather st-stut-stut-stut-stuttered a word. Then the jury was no longer as intimidated. They began listening more closely to his argument. He spoke hesitantly and honestly with a sense of respect and humility yet with knowledge and understanding. The jury ultimately ruled the case in his favor over a much more articulate, more experienced lawyer with plenty of sheen in his intellectual machine.

Even President Thomas Jefferson shunned his sheen at his inauguration. He declined to wear a ceremonial sword as the two previous US presidents had at their inaugurations. President Jefferson, rubbing the sheen off his presidential seal, also eschewed his generation's equivalent of Air Force One. He sold the 8-horse carriage and spectacular silver harness that he inherited from the previous president, John Adams.

President Jefferson's down-home sensibility even manifested itself in the White House. He would show up for dinner in his slippers and insisted on no assigned seating for his guests. He just wanted to sit and chat with you — toe to toe sort of speak— not as the well-heeled President of the United States playing a role for a formal guest. Shunning his sheen, President Jefferson made a judgment call. His authenticity was more significant than his celebrity. And his capacity for transparency heightened his ability to lead with authenticity—to advance his cause for others consistently— one foot at a time. Even in his slippers.

Mint 11

PEDIGREE
Beware & Wary of Your History

Today's EngageMINT
Remember *where*
you came from.

B lanche in *The Golden Girls* television program reminds us that our heritage casts a large shadow no matter what role you are playing: lover or leader. Blanche drawls: "I'm from the South. Flirting is part of my heritage." The most effective leaders know that your instinctive behavior, where you are initially coming from is influenced quite literally by where you come from.

And sometimes a leader can get too comfortable in his or her own familiarity, and too loose in his or her own tongue. S/he can inadvertently say something that rolls off the tongue naturally and innocently even though it could be offensive to others no matter how customary and non-threatening it is to you. That's why the most effective leaders realize their assimilated environment can foster blind spots especially when you interact with other like-minded people over time in the same geographic area. Consider President Harry S. Truman. He was born and raised in the South 20 years after the Civil War. Even as president he would privately and inadvertently refer to "niggers," according to historian David McCullough on page 588 of his biography on Truman. McCullough observed:

"On racial matters, Truman had not entirely outgrown his background. Old biases, old habits of speech continued surfacing off-stage as some of his aides and Secret Service agents would later attest. Privately, he could still speak of 'niggers' as if that were

the way one naturally referred to blacks."

Truman acknowledged his Southern heritage. He said his relatives had fought for the Confederacy in the Civil War. He noted he came from a part of Missouri where "Jim Crowism still prevailed." Truman was referring to segregationist laws mandating that Black and White patrons have separate toilet facilities, separate waiting rooms in train and bus stations, and separate entrances to restaurants. But as president, Truman also embraced his leadership role — directly and deliberately—and regularly made a concerted effort to contain his instinctive Missourian behaviors whenever he stepped in the American limelight as the Leader of the Free World.

In fact as president, Truman issued executive orders ending segregation in the military and in federal hiring practices. He became the first president to campaign in predominately Black Harlem. And he vigorously fought overt discrimination especially when a group of white Southern Democrats—his peers at one time—wrote a letter asking Truman to slow down his progressive treatment of Blacks. Truman fired back a letter that read in part:

> *"...my very stomach turned over when I learned that Negro soldiers, just back from overseas, were being dumped out of Army trucks in Mississippi and beaten. Whatever my inclinations as a native of Missouri might have been, as President, I know this is bad. I shall fight to end evils like this."*

President Truman, as an effective leader, realized that it takes a specially honed emotional intelligence to be aware of the blinders your heritage can foist on you. That's why the most effective leaders are more aware–and wary of–protecting themselves from their own DNA: Discrimination Naturally Applied. Even when they're flirting.

Mint 12

Instilling Confidence
In Troubled Times

Today's EngageMINT
*Preserve the self-confidence
of others.*

Mayday! Mayday! Mayday! The young corporate helicopter pilot screamed into the radio over Lake Michigan shortly after taking off from Chicago. Equipment failure. The blades stopped turning and the helicopter started dropping like a rock out of the sky. The pilot's heart sank just as fast. He was flying four executives on their corporate helicopter. All he could think of as he carefully and skillfully ditched the helicopter into Lake Michigan was that if he didn't die in this helicopter crash he certainly would be fired. Somebody's got to take the fall for a screw-up like this and with only two years seniority on the job he was most likely to be the fall guy.

Splash! The helicopter safely ditched and Lake Michigan quickly swallowed up the helicopter. All four executives and the pilot were safe. They were wearing their life-vests and bobbing in the 54-degree water as the sun was setting on a cool autumn day. Within an hour, the Coast Guard rescued all five. They were cold but not hurt.

The Glad-to-be-Alive-Five took other transportation that evening back to their corporate headquarters. All were back to work the following day. The next day the 28-year-old pilot got a phone call from the Boss of all bosses— the chief executive officer—who had phoned the night of the accident to make sure all of his employees were safe. The CEO asked the pilot to pick him up at the corporate headquarters in the company's backup helicopter. The pilot dutifully responded. "Where do you want to go?" asked the pilot as the CEO got in the helicopter. "Oh, nowhere in particular. Let's just go for a ride." The surprised pilot took a deep breath. His self-confidence restored, he was eventually promoted to chief pilot and his performance over the ensuing 30 years was exemplary.

The CEO did his duty as a leader. He infused a sense of self worth in another. That's what loving leaders do. They help others regain their confidence that is—loving leaders help others quite literally keep the faith—in themselves, especially when you note that the word confidence stems from the latin *(con fidere)* which means "with faith." Fostering that kind of confidence in others takes enormous compassion where loving leaders put themselves in the shoes of one of their staffers. They feel what their staffer is feeling at the moment. And they immediately demonstrate their faith and confidence in their employee especially in trying circumstances.

Of course you don't need to be a CEO to treat your colleagues with that kind of compassion: that all-consuming sense of empathy—that suffering with another—regardless how far apart you are on the organizational chart. What if you were a project leader and you personally worked on building a GLASS prototype for 24 straight hours? Then you gave your baby — your glass baby— to a staffer to carry into another testing lab. But the young intern accidentally dropped the glass into what seemed hundreds of different pieces scattered and smashed on the floor. Here's what Thomas Edison did. He rebuilt the glass light bulb prototype in another 24 hours and immediately handed the fragile bulb to the same assistant who carefully and confidently carried out the experiment flawlessly.

Lesson learned: Leaders reinforce the dignity and worth of the individual employee especially when he or she doubts themselves or is angry at themselves for screwing up. Then the most effective leaders intercede with love—a love that author and French poet Antoine de Saint Exupery defined as — the "process of my leading you back to yourself." Helicopter optional.

Mint 13

FAMILY VALUES
The Care & Feeding Of Others

Today's EngageMINT
*Shining the light on others
reflects well on you.*

Standing on a balcony overlooking the industry's most comprehensive research facility, the chief executive officer has an impressive view of his vision come alive. A photographer from The *New York Times* is setting up to take the CEO's picture commemorating the $120 million facility's official opening. The company's public relations executive is thrilled with the national exposure. But suddenly there's a snag. There's a technical issue with the photographer's lighting. The photographer asks for a few minutes to fix the lighting. The PR executive finds himself in an awkward situation: alone with the CEO with no particular meeting agenda, no proposal to be made or decision to be approved.

The taciturn CEO was at ease in the silence. However, the PR executive felt the eerie silence as if it were a weight on his shoulders. Here was his chance to impress the CEO with some gambit of pithy conversation, some insight into his expertise as the company's spokesperson, or at least some other side of his personality that would crack the CEO's wall of silence. But instead the CEO unveiled a more revealing side of his own personality.

And in the process the CEO taught the PR executive a leadership lesson in emotional intelligence in general and humility in particular, especially at a time when the CEO was deservedly perched for a lion's roar in the business jungle after a bountiful hunt in the marketplace. So bountiful that the CEO's company held a commanding lead in global sales. And now the CEO was reinforcing that leadership grip with an investment in the future. Finally the PR executive couldn't stand the awkward silence. He blurted out what came naturally to his publicity and promotion-oriented mind: "What a great tribute to your leadership and this company that the *New York Times* is here. The growth of this company in sales and employees is attracting this kind of national attention." The CEO, calm and poised in the midst of all that shower of praise, deadpanned: "What's the latest number on employees we have?

The PR executive smiled. Not only did he know the number but he was now engaged in a meaningful conversation with the chief executive officer. And he felt very good. But then the CEO donned another leadership hat and assumed another more insightful, more poignant role in redefining CEO from Chief Executive Officer to also mean Chief Emotional-Intelligence Officer.

Chief Emotional Intelligence Officer

Instead of taking a bow for his company's soaring revenues and net profit growth, the CEO as Chief Emotional-Intelligence Officer inhaled the escalating number of employees now on his payroll as if he were savoring a fine wine. He paused. His eyes widened. Then he said in a humble, matter-of-fact style devoid of any personal grandstanding: "That's a lot of families that we have fed."

Instead of stepping into the spotlight for his bow, the CEO turned the spotlight on the growth of meaningful, high-paying jobs his company produced – jobs that virtually changed the lives of thousands of his own employees and lined the pockets of thousands of other business owners in the community considering the rippling effect of those jobs on the regional economy.

No wonder on this day, the photographer's portable lighting system balked in shining a bright light on the CEO. He already stood in the reflected light of his employees.

Mint 14

Becoming a CEO:

Caring Executive Officer

Today's EngageMINT
*Step into the shoes
of your employees.*

U nder budget and on time. The project team leader confirmed that the new company softball diamond would be ready for the season opener. No wonder the project team leader was feeling proud of his team's accomplishment as he drove up to the field a few days before the first game to do a final inspection. But then he felt like someone had kicked him in the stomach. "Bleachers! Who ordered those bleachers?" No one knew. Finally the team leader rushed into the CEO's office, knowing he had failed to stay under budget, knowing that it will seem to the CEO and other decision makers at this billion-dollar, privately-held company that he was deliberately lying to make his numbers look good.

The project team leader was in crisis mode to save face. He had to be the first to tell the CEO that someone spent unauthorized dollars on his project. "I don't know who authorized this but I will get to the bottom of this," the team leader huffed to the CEO. "I had this under control. I swear. I will find out who did this to me." The CEO tried to calm the team leader down, reassuring him that everything would be all right. "I know who purchased those bleachers," the CEO said.

The project team leader fell silent and perched on his seat to figuratively pounce on whatever name fell from the lips of the CEO. "I did. You can't expect family and friends to sit on the ground." The project team leader sat back in his seat and smiled. The CEO had taught him a valuable leadership lesson. Budgets are important but so are people. The project team leader did his job staying under budget on the approved project. And the CEO did his job, focusing on the second bottom line of trust and loyalty and long-term commitment to his employees. That day, the project team leader realized that CEO stands for much more than Chief Executive Officer. Maybe it also stands for Caring Executive Officer albeit as touchy and feely as that sounds. Still, the most effective CEOs realize that anything they can do to make the lives of their employees and their families more viable— the more they can fortify their employee family— the more productive their workforce and the more loyal their commitment to the company. And profits will follow.

That's why CEOs—Caring Executive Officers—feel their way to the bottom line one employee at a time. They feel what their people feel. They roll up their sleeves and offer to help clear away the clutter in their employee's lives. Sometimes that even means physically wielding a broom or carrying a box or two especially after a big event. Are you kidding me? A CEO has more important things to do than help a staffer pack up after a press conference.

Yet after meeting privately with the Governor in the state Capitol, the CEO stopped by the room where the press conference had taken place. The CEO saw his PR guy gathering up the presentation boards and other materials used in the press conference. The CEO matter-of-factly asked his PR guy if he needed any help packing up the press conference materials. "No, sir, I've got this," the surprised PR guy answered. The governor's press aide stood in awe as the CEO left the room. "Did that just happen?" the governor's press aide mumbled. "That's a first."

That sense of empathy from a CEO for the awareness of the rigors of the daily grind on and off the job in general and the everyday responsibilities of their employees reinforces the trusting and caring relationships than anchors a leader's success. In his book *Executive Warfare*, the former CEO of John Hancock Financial Services David D'Alessandro cautions: "Make sure you never forget that most lives involve a lot of struggle because people will not look up to you if you have no empathy for them." On the job or even at a softball game.

Mint 15

Loving Your Retirees
With Dignity & Respect

Today's EngageMINT

*Be there in person to celebrate
the anniversary of long-term relationships.*

Shocked! The highly-recruited and newly-appointed CEO was shocked and perplexed when the Chairman of the company left an urgent message for the CEO to curtail his European business trip and return as soon as possible to the corporate headquarters in the United States. Was it an unwanted takeover bid? Or a kidnapping of a board member? The new CEO, the first to take over command of the privately-held company from outside the family in nearly 90 years, wondered what the crisis was about as he hurriedly broke away from negotiations to acquire a company that would shore up a vulnerability in the company's product line.

With a sense of anxiety and nervous curiosity, the new CEO called the Chairman. He listened and then sighed in a frustrating and exasperating tone. "A party—a retirement party?" the new CEO repeated. "You want me to leave millions of dollars on the table right now—that's the potential we have in acquiring this company that we had already talked about with you and the Board—to fly back to corporate headquarters to attend a retirement party? The Chairman of the Board calmly and resolutely confirmed his direction. The new CEO acquiesced. Under duress, the new CEO did attend the retirement party—an annual event that celebrates, lauds and says a big Thank You to hundreds of current employees with 25 years or more of service and attracts hundreds of retired employees some of whom accumulated 30-40 years of service to the company. That annual Retirement Party, celebrated for more than four decades, is so important that top management including the Chairman and the CEO and each company president made it their ritual each year to be there in person to shake as many hands as possible of the people who quite literally grew their company. The new CEO, recruited from another global company, never understood the critical importance of top management attending the Retirement Party. He had the Retirement Party on his calendar as optional. Two months later, the Chairman fired the new CEO because of their "philosophical differences" according the company's news release. What happened?

Enlightened Leaders
Say Thank You

The new CEO thought he could make the company's wheel spin more efficiently with another spoke—an acquisition—rather than focusing on what really makes a wheel stronger: the space between those spokes, the space where relationships foster, the space where mutual caring and respect foment and the space where the dignity and worth of each individual is celebrated regardless of their role in the company. That space between the spokes is filled with respect by top management for their employees both current and former. And those loyal employees look forward to basking in the glow of that respect, that appreciation, that love from top management that nurtures their personal pride in their work in particular and their commitment to the company in general.

To the rank and file, that recognition from top management felt so genuine, so real when they could look into the eyes of the owners of the privately-held company and feel their sincerity in saying "Thank you" so personally and so poignantly. Many among the thousand or so current and retired employees at the Retirement Party were amazed at how the CEO could remember their names (and sometimes even their spouse's name) even though they had met ONLY ONCE before years ago. That's what loving leaders do. They know their people first as people then as employees. Those enlightened leaders recognize that it is the space (the people) between the spokes (new products, acquisitions) that turns the wheels consistently in their company. They are well aware that two sets of spokes of identical strength do not necessarily make wheels of identical strength. Engineers note that the strength of a wheel is also affected by the spaces between the spokes and therefore the spaces are critically important in the overall performance as philosopher Lao-Tse observed:

> *"Thirty spokes meet in the hub but the empty space between them is the essence of the wheel.*
>
> *"Pots are formed from clay but the empty space within it is the essence of the pot.*
>
> *"Walls with windows and doors form the house but the empty space within is the essence of the house.*
>
> *"And so we see advantage is had from whatever is there but usefulness rises from whatever is not."*

Indeed, usefulness in a wheel stems from whatever is not there—the spaces—between the spokes. It is that space that ultimately determines the strength of each spoke. Those strength-building spaces emanating from the hub of the wheel are much like the umbilical cord in a human that is so critical to the strength, vitality and viability of an unborn baby. In fact, the hub of the wheel is called the "nave" as in navel. This belly-button of sorts at the hub reinforces the interdependence between the spaces and the spokes that ultimately turns the wheel. Both need each other.

Significantly, the focus is always first on the spaces—on the followers—not on the spokes, not on the leaders. A leader is sanctioned only when others follow in much the same way a wheel will spin only when the spaces (followers) are correctly aligned to support the spokes (the leader). That's why Keith Grint, a professor of public leadership at Warwick University in Coventry, England, notes: "In short, the power of leaders is a consequence of the actions of followers rather than a cause of it. In effect, leadership is the property and the consequence of a community rather than of an individual." Even a community of retired employees—a trans-Atlantic flight away—no matter how hot and juicy the business grill is at the time. It comes down to much more than the vision you have for your company. It comes down to your followers' line of sight more than simply your insight. That's why the most effective leaders know their vision has to be shared personally from the side and acclaimed by all constituents rather than simply proclaimed from the top.

Making Eye Contact
Up Close & Personal

From the side — up close and personal with their followers—a leader can more accurately assess key components of a vision such as competition, customers and employees. From the side, a leader can come to more directly experience their company's strengths and weaknesses in the marketplace. From the side, a leader can more fully listen to what the employee and/or customer is NOT saying that would enhance the value-add of their product or service.   And from the side—up close and personal with their followers—a leader can more sincerely look their employees and customers in the eye to gain and retain their trust.

But first, the leader's view from the side has to be tailored to a specific angle so that others can see what the leader sees—much like the specific 42-degree angle of vision required to see a rainbow, according to the laws of physics. No wonder the most effective visionary leaders realize their followers may have a similar lookout point but not share the same vantage point on issues affecting the company. Managers see the spokes. Employees see the space between the spokes. And leaders align both points of view with that precise angle so that both can focus on their "rainbow" and personally sense more meaning and relevancy to their collective vision.

That's why the most effective visionary leaders set "the context for other people so they can make good decisions, judgement calls and tradeoffs on a moment by moment basis without having to ask someone every time," notes Jennifer Chatman, Professor of Management at the Haas Business School at the University of California, Berkeley. "That's when you get groups firing on all cylinders." And that's when you get visionary leaders balancing both the spokes—and the space between the spokes—to keep the wheels turning and still keep the rainbow in focus.

Mint 16

R-E-S-P-E-C-T
Putting the Spell on Others

Today's EngageMINT
Respect all especially those
who disrespect you.

Belligerent, the fuming teenager couldn't contain himself any longer: "You bitch!" he erupted, firing his his words with a glaring vile toward a veteran officer at the Juvenile Detention Center. Darlene, poised and confident, paused. She looked deep into the glowering eyes of her verbal attacker, his pulsating veins dancing frantically in his neck.

"Now just a minute," Darlene shot back, firing her words like bullets between the eyes of the teenager. "Have I ever called you anything but your given name? Have I ever shown you any disrespect for who you are as a person? What gives you the right to call me anything but my given name?" The teenager lowered his eyes and lowered his voice. "Yeah, yeah," he grumbled and mumbled more to himself than anyone else. The anger-filled veins in his neck slowed their dance from a reggae to a ballet. "Yeah, yeah," he repeated. Darlene's eyes beamed a warm glow on him that he felt more than he saw from the Juvenile Detention Center officer.

The teenager walked out of that gymnasium at the detention center, leaving behind much more than his anger. He felt different. More confident. Less arrogant. More disciplined. Less defiant. The teenager couldn't remember when anyone told him they would never disrespect him as a person. Suddenly Aretha Franklin's voice popped into his head. She is singing "R-E-S-P-E-C-T" echoing the Juvenile Detention Center officer's admonition that respect begets respect. Darlene demonstrated a key leadership skill: Love the sinner; hate the sin. Darlene could have reacted to the teenager with her own passionate barrage of verbal abuse or authoritarian measures. Darlene could have taken charge of that situation. But loving leaders do not have to TAKE charge. They are always IN CHARGE of themselves. They are always IN CHARGE of treating others with dignity and respect and influencing others to behave productively. And as a leader, Darlene finds the more she respects others, the more they respect her over time. In fact research at the University of Kansas reaffirms Darlene's leadership effectiveness. In that study, mothers kept track of how often they paid attention to their problem children's good behavior. As the mothers became more supportive the children's behaviors improved.

The Shape Is Already
In The Stone

Leaders pay attention to others. They see more than meets the eye. They see beneath that rock-solid exterior that some hide behind. They see the faces of integrity invariably beaming through the hardened and sullied rock in the same way the sculptor saw the 60-foot tall faces of George Washington, Abraham Lincoln, Thomas Jefferson and Teddy Roosevelt long before he took the first chisel to Mount Rushmore. Sculptor Gutzon Borglum said he removed unwanted rock and brought out the best of what was already there. He echoed the sentiments of Michelangelo who said before creating his *David* that "the shape is already in the stone."

Loving leaders like sculptors know that the potential and creative energy of their people are already in the "stone." Likewise, Darlene reinforced the leadership tenet that everyone has value even if it is hidden deep below the surface, clouded in circumstance or buried in bigotry. As Andrew Carnegie once said: "You develop people in the same way you mine for gold. In the gold mine you move tons of dirt to find an ounce of gold. You don't look for the dirt. You look for the gold." Especially when someone first calls you a "bitch."

Mint 17

Feeding Others
Food For The Soul

●

Today's EngageMINT
*Respect the personal & political
rights of your employees.*

You're a nobody. At least you feel that way as a third stringer. You're sitting on the sidelines of life. You will never get in the game. No one ever cheers for you. No one ever champions you. No one ever seems to care about you. Then suddenly you find yourself sitting in first class. Even the first stringers—the stars—defer to you. Dreaming? No. Leading with class. Take it from a highly successful leader – Bo Schembechler – former head football coach at the University of Michigan. On charter flights to away games, Schembechler reserved all 20 seats in first class for senior football players. No coaches. No alumni. No fat cats. Just seniors. No matter if you played third string. And no matter if you were a highly recruited top player but NOT yet a senior. The first class treatment for the senior class players sent a clear message:

> *We value hard work over time and even if you're not one of the top players on the team, you've earned our respect.*

How do you pay respect to your rank and file employees over the long-term? Of course you can't give everyone a financial reward or first class seats on an airplane. But you can make your people feel especially appreciated. Consider this example of giving others the first class treatment when a product development team was working under deadline pressure. The executives of the software company felt hopeless. They didn't write code. The fate of this project was now in the hands of computer programmers working late into the night. The executives decided they could help. They dressed like formal servers — bow tie and all— as in a five-star restaurant and then personally served a catered dinner to each of the 14 programmers working late that night. The development team got the message and their customers got the product shipped on time. Servant leaders TAKE orders more than issue them. And food is often a cost-effective and much appreciated tool to engage your workforce. That's why supervisors in thousands of manufacturing plants host a cookout and serve their employees much more than food for their stomachs. They serve them food for the soul: respect and gratitude. That's why Navy officers aboard a guided missile destroyer no longer could pull rank in the food line, according to Captain D. Michael Abrashoff, writing in his book *It's Your Ship*. The Navy officers stood in the back of the line like everyone else recognizing their equality as human beings doing a very human thing: eating.

Respecting the Political Privacy of Your Employees

Loving leaders resist their basic instincts to pull rank in matters that have nothing to do with the operations of the company. They realize treating others first class means also respecting their personal privacy. Consider the CEO who turned down a request from the President of the United States to conduct a campaign rally at the company's corporate headquarters building. Virtually all of his company vice presidents favored the opportunity for the company to step into the national spotlight and reach new potential customers especially since the candidate's message resonated well with the values of the company. Yet, the CEO said he turned down the campaign request out of respect for the company's employees who may have a different political view. The CEO said it was his duty to respect the view of all of his employees. But some complained that the CEO had let his own politics blunt an opportunity for his company to enhance its marketing punch and broaden its profitability margin. But the CEO demurred: "My Republican friends think I am a Democrat and my Democrat friends think I am a Republican." Turns out the CEO, like all loving leaders, see themselves as just another employee serving other employees with respect and treating all of them with class. First class.

Mint 18

Make Someone Feel Important Today

●

Today's EngageMINT
*Hang proverbial mistletoe
in your office.*

You and your significant other attend a Christmas party and find yourselves appropriately positioned under the mistletoe draping the doorway. You both realize the traditional opportunity no matter how quaint and old-fashioned it seems yet both of you enjoy the obligatory kiss. Imagine the effect of—and affect on—the working environment if there were a figurative mistletoe hanging in the office of a leader. That's not as preposterous as it seems. At least not to the loving leader who positioned a plaque in his office so that he could see it on the wall directly behind the head of his visitor: *Make Someone Feel Important Today.* That plaque reminded the leader that in conferring with a visitor or direct report to pay attention to the feelings as much as the facts their discussion evinced.

The office version of mistletoe helped the leader slow down to focus as much on the person as on the problem. It's too easy to get caught up in the hustle and bustle of the office — just like it's too easy to get caught up in the hustle and bustle of Christmas time at home until you step under mistletoe hung strategically over a doorway and take a time-out. Standing under that mistletoe, you pause, look into your partner's eyes, kiss and make each other feel important. No matter how busy you are. No matter how mad you are. No matter how exhausted you are.

That's why The Make-Someone-Feel-Important-Today plaque was situated so strategically. The leader could maintain eye contact with his or her visitor and simultaneously maintain a clear view of the message on the plaque behind the head of his visitor: *Make Someone Feel Important Today.* Loving leaders make people feel important in good and bad times. They celebrate their joys, stir their dreams and embody the inherent wisdom in the observation of the founder of Mary Kay Cosmetics that people want recognition and praise more than money or sex.

Making someone's day better is "contagious and increases the energy, effectiveness and productivity in any organization," notes CEO Joel Manby in his book *Love Works.* Even hard-charging, discipline-oriented football coaches can foster that contagious sense of caring that increases the energy, effectiveness and productivity of a player. Just ask Willie Davis, one of the star professional football players on Coach Vince Lombardi's Green Bay Packers. As soon as Davis found out that Lombardi was dying in a hospital, the former defensive end who played on two Lombardi-coached, Super Bowl- winning teams took the next flight from Los Angeles to Washington. The media asked Davis why he would fly across the country just for a few minutes with Lombardi in the hospital. "He always made me feel so very important, so very valued, so good about myself," Davis said. "I just had to see him one more time before he died."

That's what leaders do. They make others feel important. They pay attention to others even if they have to hang their own office version of mistletoe to remind them to take a time-out. They pause and really look into each other's eyes. They really hear what each other is saying. They really sense what each other is feeling. And they really touch each other's humanity with a proverbial kiss that provides each other much more than lip service. They feel appreciated, valued and loved. And they parlay that caring mindset into even more caring performance on the job.

*"More than money
or sex, people want
recognition and praise."*

**Mary Kay Ash,
founder, Mary Kay Cosmetics**

Mint 19

Saying 'I'm Sorry'
The Write Way

Today's EngageMINT
*Card your employees
with a Hallmark Helper.*

My new boss had my back. "I'll be there to give you moral support," he told me as I prepared for a presentation the next morning at a large sales meeting. It really didn't matter that my boss never showed. He clearly had confidence in me. Besides, the presentation went well as expected. As soon as I got back to the office, my boss stopped me before I even had a chance to sit down. He looked at me and said contritely: "I screwed up. I just forgot all about it. I am sorry. So sorry. That's for you."

My boss pointed to an envelope on my desk. The envelope had my name written in perfect penmanship. Inside there was a motivational card that said "Challenge" on the front. I opened the card and read his carefully handwritten apology. I knew my new boss as a highly successful leader who had brandished his reputation as street-smart, don't-mess-with-me guy for more than 30 years at the same company. That's why I felt goose bumps sprinkle all over my neck as I read his words: "I'm sorry. I screwed up...."

Each letter he wrote in his best penmanship seemed so thoughtfully scripted, so poignantly inscribed. His expensive fountain pen seemed to ooze drops like so many virtual tears. His words seemed so genuine, so sincere that I needed to swallow before getting back to work. Then I thought how easily he could have hidden behind the managerial code for screwing up: *"I had another emergency that I had to handle right away and couldn't get over to your meeting."* But he didn't. He just simply confessed. He admitted his mistake. My boss's apology—in person and in writing—really touched me and rekindled my commitment to him personally and to our company collectively. From that day of the apology going forward, I seemed to bring my "A" game to the office much more often. I felt like I was more productive. Maybe I was just working longer rather than smarter. Not sure. But I figured if my new boss cared that much about me, I should care even more about making him look good in hiring me in the first place.

My new boss-turned-pen-pal taught me a significant leadership lesson that day. It's a lesson that has served me well in developing teams and building trust over the years. Value the dignity and worth of your team. Be true to your word, especially if you are vowing support – materially, physically or spiritually. And if that bond of trust is broken, be quick, vocal, and verbal in apologizing personally. Then document your apology with your signature statement. It's one thing to perfunctorily mouth the words —"I'm sorry"— and call it good. It's another thing to sit down, swallow your pride and your positional authority. Then take the time to search for a Hallmark Helper (inspirational cards); write out your apology and then personally deliver it.

That Pen-Pal approach in apologizing first in writing and then face-to-face takes enormous emotional intelligence backed with a well-executed plan of caring. No click does the trick. No hiding behind E-mail. No texting. After all, your ability to write is uniquely human. And the act of writing in your longhand is particularly personal, so personal that those few drops of ink spread like so much DNA from your hand that no machine can perfectly match your signature. Just ask any celebrity autograph seeker. That's why loving leaders stock inspirational blank greeting cards in their offices the way others stock business cards. At least that's what I later discovered about my boss. Chances are pretty good that I was not the first—nor the last of his direct reports—to be "carded."

Mint 20

CHARISMA:
Helping Others Feel Comfortable

Today's EngageMINT
Infuse others to like themselves
when you're around.

Marilyn Monroe, the flashy, sassy actress of the 1950s, was an introvert who could climb out of her shell when she needed to influence others. She found a way to make others feel good about themselves no matter how uncomfortable she felt about shedding her introvert's security blanket. And in the process Marilyn Monroe demonstrated a key understanding about charisma:

> **Charisma is not**
> **something you have.**
> **It's something you give**
> **to your audience.**

"Being charismatic means making others feel comfortable, at ease and good about themselves," observes author Olivia Fox Cabane in her book *The Charisma Myth*. Cabane notes that Norma Jean Dougherty— Marilyn's given name—could sit anonymously like any other introvert on a crowded train. But once she reached her destination, she would unleash her charisma: her eyes flashing, her voice cooing, her hips swiveling to make her audience in general and the *paparazzi* in particular feel even more comfortable around her. She acted so that others would more readily react favorably to her and feel more comfortable around her as a person beyond her sensuality in general and flirting in particular. How do leaders generate that kind of charisma that affects and reflects off others especially if you don't look like a movie star or aren't as glib as a talk show host? Relax. Be yourself. Be real. Smile. Hone your eye contact. Express interest in others. Lean in when you listen to someone. And realize that your charisma springs from the integrity of your heart and soul more than from the tone of your voice or your command of the language. Research shows that charisma "is the result of specific non-verbal behaviors not an inherent or magical personal quality," writes Cabane in her book *The Charisma Myth.* "One of the most interesting research findings is that you can be a very charismatic introvert."

Charm
Can Harm

Charisma, once thought the province of the chosen few, is available to all who counter-intuitively focus their energy toward others and their well-being. Think of charisma as a light you shine on others and then bask in its glow. Consider President Ronald Reagan who was "essentially a loner, but when he was around a camera and an audience, he would light up, his juices flowing, eager to talk," observed author David Gergen in his book *Eyewitness To Power.*

But overdone, the Hollywood-style of charisma (all sizzle and no steak) can harm more than it charms. In fact charisma can be viewed as a liability in determining the most effective leaders — Level 5—in the parlance of Jim Collins in his book *Good to Great* where humility reigns over hubris and caring and sharing are more valued than sartorial splendor or oratorical flair. Management expert Rosabeth Moss Kanter agrees. Writing in the *Harvard Business Review,* Kanter says that inevitably it's the over-the-top charismatic extroverted leader who gets into trouble either personally or gets the organization into difficulty.

However in humbly acknowledging others and listening to their concerns, loving leaders inherently make others feel more comfortable around them. Their charisma shines a spotlight on their followers who feel more empowered in decision making, more comfortable in working up to their potential and more committed to profitable and productive results.

PART II

CONNECTION

*"In every office you hear
the threads of love and joy
and fear and guilt,
the cries for celebration
and reassurance.*

*"And somehow
you know
connecting those threads
is what you are supposed to do.*

*"And business
takes care of itself."*

-Jim Autry, Author,
Love and Profit

Mint 21

GOOSING
The Goose Bumps

Today's EngageMINT
Empathize with the
feelings of others.

After four years of marriage, Debbie was thrilled that at last she might be pregnant. She was so excited when she stepped into the examination room at her doctor's office. However, after the exam her doctor seemed to forget that she was still in the room. He looked over to the attending nurse and reported in a clinical drone: "The cervix is blue. That indicates pregnancy." The obstetrician made a feint attempt at eye contact with his patient. Then he brusquely left the examination room and hurried off to his next patient. Debbie felt abandoned on her first trip to Mommy Land. She expected at least a warm inviting smile. She got only a cold dismissive shoulder. No way. No how. She fumed.

A few days later Debbie saw another doctor. He conducted a similar examination with similar results but with a decidedly different response. The doctor shook Debbie's hand and beamed: "Congratulations, congratulations, you are going to have a baby!" Debbie beamed. She felt goose bumps running down her back. She was so elated. So thrilled. So fulfilled.

Goosing the goose bumps—triggering a sense of well-being in others—is a critical skill for the most loving leaders and engaged employees. When feelings more than just the facts are shared, trust soars and mutual understanding and confidence ensues in any relationship particularly one as intimate as doctor/patient. With feelings comes a human bond that cements conviction and leads to outstanding service, quality, performance and bottom-line impact. For example, doctors are sued less often if they demonstrate more of a listening posture and caring protocol in their initial meeting with the patient, research confirms. And that more caring posture enhances results since the art of medicine in part "consists of amusing the patient while nature cures the disease," as Voltaire observed. That's why loving leaders find ways of tapping into the feelings of others, of "amusing" their followers and goosing their goose bumps to more readily grease the wheels of success, according to Jim Autry, a former chief executive officer of a multi-million dollar company. In his book, *Love and Profit*, Autry writes:

> *"In every office you hear the threads*
> *of love and joy and fear and guilt,*
> *the cries for celebration and reassurance.*
>
> *"And somehow you know*
> *connecting those threads is*
> *what you are supposed to do.*
> *And business takes care of itself."*

How do you connect those threads? With a sharpened emotional intelligence. With a high degree of paying attention to how you feel and with a high degree of paying even more attention to how others around you feel particularly under stress, according to Daniel Goleman, author of *Emotional Intelligence*. He calls emotional intelligence the "sine qua non" of leadership. That means that emotional intelligence is an essential condition of leadership. The Latin phrase (sine qua non) means "without which nothing."

So without emotional intelligence, there can be no leadership. That's why The Center for Creative Leadership found that "insensitivity to others" is the most cited reason that leaders fail. And that sensitivity to others—that feeling for the feelings of others—is the essence of the long-term impact of the most influential leaders. As poet Maya Angelou noted: "People will forget what you said. People will forget what you did. But people will always remember how you made them feel."

Mint 22

AFFIRM
Long Before You Inform

Today's EngageMINT
Acknowledge the initial reality
others are facing.

Bleeding and screaming, the 5-year-old girl tries in vain to fend off her growling attackers after she inadvertently wandered into a pit-bull dog pen. Her mother, panicking at the screams, swoops into the pen like a hawk. She sweeps up her frightened and bitten daughter into the safety of her arms. "Ssh, Ssh, Ssh, it's okay now," her mom coos. She rushes her daughter to the security of a nearby bench, far away from the now locked dog pen. "You're okay. Momma's here for you. Ssh, Ssh, Ssh."

But to no avail.

Her little girl continues to cry. The louder her mom tries to comfort her daughter with an affectionate "Ssh, Ssh," the louder she cries. And the more she cries the more she bleeds. The crying and bleeding seemed to get worse just when the ambulance arrived. The trained medical first responder took the opposite tact.

First, he confronted the situation. Then he comforted the victim. The medical first responder first confirmed her reality of the situation as the frightened and injured little girl had just experienced it. "Wow, look at all that blood on your arm. I'll bet that really hurts, doesn't it?"

Then the medical first responder knelt down and looked into the little girl's tearful eyes and gently asked: "Can you help me?" The little girl nodded. Her screaming diminished. "I think together we can stop that blood," he said calmly and confidently while handing the girl a compress. "Just press this down on your arm while I bandage your other arm, okay? The girl took the compress pad. She stopped screaming. He held the injured girl's arm as she pressed the bandage. "Hey you are doing a great job for me," he said in an assuring tone. "I knew you could stop that blood and you did!" Soon her bleeding stopped. So did her crying.

The little girl was in the caring hands of a loving leader, a trained first responder who knew that the way to initially treat a trauma victim is to first retreat into their world, to see the situation from their eyes, to feel their pain as they are feeling it.

Validating Others

In initially confronting her reality more than simply comforting her feelings, the first responder did much more than persuade the girl to stop crying. He influenced her to process her feelings; to make sense of her feelings, and ultimately to take control over her feelings. But most of all he validated her feelings and reinforced her self-worth.

Expressing his emotional intelligence with more other-directed empathy than self-serving sympathy, this loving leader validated her feelings and in the process validated her. Then together they validated a process, working together—care giver and care recipient—to regain stability and create a new reality.

That's what leaders do. They help others cope and hope without discounting the reality of the situation or diminishing the impact of the circumstances NOW. No matter how vicious the proverbial dogs.

To Treat a Trauma Victim,
First Retreat
Into Their World.

Mint 23

INTIMACY
Baring Yourself To Learn From Others

Today's EngageMINT
Show interest in the
personal lives of your employees.

Anna's song in the Broadway play *The King and I* — *"Getting to Know You, Getting to Know All About You"* —could be the anthem of the most effective leaders. They embrace the research that says the MOST important leadership skill is taking a sincere personal interest in your employees. There's a bottom-line, performance-driven significance to that Getting-to-Know-You/Seeking-to-Understand-You focus on followers. And the most effective leaders leverage that understanding of individual differences into well integrated, highly productive teams that can achieve outstanding results like doubling the size of the United States, according to historian Stephen Ambrose.

In his book *Undaunted Courage,* Ambrose notes that Captain Meriwether Lewis and Second Lieutenant William Clark of the U.S. Army developed "outstanding leadership" with their Getting-to-Know-You/Seeking-to-Understand-You initiatives with their team of 35 volunteers who explored and mapped the Louisiana Purchase, the body of land from what is now Missouri to California acquired from France in 1804. During their 7,000-mile expedition Lewis & Clark developed what Ambrose called an "intimate" insight into each team person's skills and behavioral tendencies long before instruments such as the Kolbe Index.

That insight evolved "into a tough, superbly disciplined family" which fostered a caring and sharing working environment that encouraged others to perform intimately at their best. The dictionary defines intimate as "a warm friendship developed through a long association." That warm friendship is not the buddy-buddy, let's-have-a-beer together friendship. This is a workplace relationship that puts work in its place—in context. To get intimate, leaders have to figuratively bare themselves in front of their followers. They virtually disrobe. They hide nothing. They become even more vulnerable. And they learn so much more about themselves and others.

The more the leader reveals about herself or himself personally, the more their followers are likely to follow their lead. Then progressively, the more their followers disclose meaningful tendencies in their own heart and soul the more a leader can better leverage that personal information for their mutual benefit. Ultimately when the most loving leaders and engaged employees come to know each other even more "intimately" they can better execute the fundamental act of a leader, according to historian and Pulitzer-prize winning author James MacGregor Burns in his seminal book *Leadership*:

"The leader's fundamental act
is to induce people to be aware
or conscious of what they feel,
to feel their true needs so strongly,
to define their values so meaningfully,
that they can be moved
to purposeful action."

Loving leaders know it is more productive for them to understand their followers than it is for their followers to understand them, as author Garry Wills notes in his book *Certain Trumpets*. Moving people to purposeful action begins with the Getting-to- Know-You /Seeking-to-Understand-You mantra as author Dale Carnegie observed in his iconic book, *How to Win Friends and Influence People*. The more you as the leader are intimately interested in your team — in their lives in and out of work— the more your team will be interested in your interests, in your mission, in your vision both personally and professionally. And the more your team will better align their talents to grow the bottom line.

Mint 24

BEE-ing a Leader:

Pollinating Others

●

Today's EngageMINT
Visit with each of your direct reports
first thing every day at their workstation.

Alice, diligently running her machine in the busy factory, heard her name blared out over the din. She stepped away from her machine as her boss approached. "Hi, Alice, how did Sarah do in the dance recital yesterday?" Alice's face lit up. Instantly she forgot how tired she was. Alice relived the joy and sheer sense of accomplishment she experienced at her daughter's dance recital. That empowering question from her leader made Alice feel like an even more important member of the factory team, valued more as a person for their heart and soul more than just another pair of hands.

Then of course when the conversation turned to more business issues on current work load or work flow both the leader and Alice knew they had invested a higher degree of trust and credibility in each other, a trust that would enhance their working relationship and more positively impact her job performance and the company's bottom line. That trust, anchored in a personal and sincere interest in each other, fosters more accurate, more timely information to solve problems, curb costs, reinforce the influence of a leader and enhance the productivity of the employee.

Employees who feel they are listened to and have daily access to you, are less likely to exercise their Open Door rights to complain about you. That's why the most effective leaders invest in the Friendly Five every day when they devote at least five minutes to personally visiting with each of their employees and talking about their personal issues first and work-related issues second. Loving leaders know that if they spend a few minutes first thing each day visiting with each of their direct reports at their workstation—virtually taking their temperature—they will more fully assess the fluid working environment in time to preempt at least a few problems and increase morale. And they will be better able to align talent and leverage resources to on-going changes for greater productivity and profitability.

Focusing on
The Friendly Five

Think of yourself as a bee pollinating flowers every morning when you make your Friendly Five rounds. That's the way Walt Disney characterized his leadership style. Disney compared himself to a bumble bee "going from one area in the studio to another to stimulate everybody." Pollinating the blossoming of others is an instructive metaphor for the essence of a loving leader. No wonder the most effective leaders schedule no formal meetings for at least the first hour "in the office."

Instead, these Busy Bees of another kind are busy flapping their proverbial wings in a series of impromptu interactions, assessing the heart count long before the head count and learning more about the dance recitals and ball games before evaluating the business reports and daily production schedules. As motivational speaker and author Zig Ziglar said: "If you help enough people get what they need, you will get what you want." In helping others get what they need, some leaders say they can save themselves six hours of headaches every day with just two hours invested first thing every morning conducting their Friendly Five. Then you have the rest of the day to do what you do best: lead. Proactively. Pre-emptively. Progressively.

The leadership lesson is clear: To galvanize their leading role, loving leaders make sure they let their direct reports give them a PIECE of their mind at the start of their day. Then both the leader and his or her staff can enjoy more peace of mind throughout the rest of the day.

Mint 25

Cozying Up To a Lizard Named Sam

Today's EngageMINT
*We're all connected
no matter how different we are.*

Carefully displaying a lizard for the general public at a zoo, the rancher eyed a woman in the front row. Suddenly she backed away. "I don't like reptiles," she demurred.

"It's not a reptile. It's a lizard," the rancher said.

The woman winced at the implied distinction without a difference. Then the rancher lifted his lizard like a trophy for all to see. In a soft, comforting voice that seemed to caress the on-lookers as he focused on the lizard's face, he whispered: "His name is Sam." Then the rancher paused, scanned the crowd and finally broke the silence saying, "Lizards aren't so bad when you get to know their names." He looked at the same woman in the audience and said, "Do you want to pet Sam now? Her wince transformed into a smile. The rancher and Sam the Lizard demonstrated how getting to know someone more personally—even their first name—can shine a more inviting light to leverage their differences for their mutual growth.

That's what loving leaders do. They focus on R-Rated leadership—R for Relationships. In building relationships, leaders more fully realize their value to each other and their connection with each other. They know that we are all connected, that what happens to one of us happens to all of us. They know for whom the bell tolls. They know it tolls for all of us as English poet John Donne asserted in his *Meditation XVII:* "Any man's death diminishes me, because I am involved in mankind, and therefore never send to know for whom the bell tolls; it tolls for thee." For thee. For you and me. Collectively. "No man is an island of itself," Donne asserted. So when that bell rings in a collaborative community, the loving leader's commitment to others broadens and their connection to each other strengthens. Consider the we-need-each-other message that Governor John Winthrop advocated before the colonists landed in Massachusetts Bay Colony in 1630.

> *"We must delight in each other, make others conditions our own, rejoice together, mourn together, labor and suffer together. We must always have before our eyes our community as members of the same body."*

Fostering community. That's what leaders do. They collaborate. They corroborate. They cooperate. They face the issues together—head on. Face to face.

Loving leaders become more self-less and less selfish. They say "I am sorry" more. They say "thank you" even more often. And they sharpen their sight and hearing to more fully consider the connective tissue that too often can bind and blind us as Pulitzer-Prize winning musician Bob Dylan sings in his song *Blowin' in the Wind*:

> *"How many times must a man look*
> *up before he can see the sky?*
> *How many ears must one man have*
> *before he can hear people cry?"*

Indeed, loving leaders listen first where the other is coming from more than simply where they're from. And they seek first to understand what the other is like more than simply what they look like.

Especially if he is lizard. Named Sam.

INVESTING

In Your Team's Mutual Trust Fund

●

Today's EngageMINT
*Build trust on the
Rock of Relationships
cemented over time.*

You're a General leading a battle when you're forced to surrender to an even more immediate lethal enemy: a fever-maddening illness that threatens your life. You are so sick that even your cadre of official physicians refuse to treat you. They are scared. They fear they will be cited for negligence or even murder. And it gets worse. Compounding your predicament, you learn of a rumor that your rival is offering a reward to assassinate you.

Finally you solicit a doctor willing to treat you against the odds. But then just as you begin to take the medicine this doctor just prepared for you, a messenger delivers a letter with an urgent warning. The letter says the medicine you are about to drink is poison. The letter also warns that your doctor has been paid off by a rival General to assassinate you.

What do you do? You do what Alexander the Great did. He scanned the letter and immediately swallowed the medicine as cavalierly as if he were downing a beer. Then he immediately handed the note to the doctor. The doctor also read the inflammatory note and hardly reacted to being called an assassin. He knew better. And so did Alexander the Great. Truth conquers all, especially the truth honed over a long-term relationship rooted in two-way communication of listening to each other rather than speaking at one another.

Alexander the Great had invested in a long term relationship with Philip of Acarnania who served as his physician when Alexander was a boy. He knew this Dr. Phil of Yesteryear would honor his Hippocratic Oath: *"Do No Harm."* He trusted him. They had invested in each other over the years with something more valuable and more valued than simply cash in their Mutual Trust Fund. They each had invested the currency of their character, the currency of their commitment, and the currency of their personal and professional conviction over time. The doctor's willingness to treat his patient and Alexander's eagerness to seek medical treatment in this precarious situation illustrates that trust is "the great accelerator," according to Shawn Moon and Sue Dathe-Douglass in their book, *The Ultimate Competitive Advantage,* "where everything is faster and less complicated and where trust is low, everything is slower, costlier and encumbered with suspicion." Dr. Phil of Yesteryear's trusting response demonstrates that trust—The Great Accelerator—is more correctly used as a verb not a noun.

- *Trust like empathy is something you DO for others—not something you demand from others.*
- *Trust like empathy is something you GIVE to others—not something you demand from others.*

That's why loving leaders find that investing in a Mutual Trust Fund with their constituents requires regular deposits over a long-term relationship that builds trust especially in adverse conditions. Developing that kind of trusting relationship demands persistent and consistent hard work between the leader and his constituents. Trust is built on the Rock of Relationships cemented over time. As Max De Pree notes in his book *Leading without Power:*

> *"Earning trust is not easy, nor is it cheap, nor does it happen quickly. Earning trust is hard and demanding work. Trust comes only with genuine effort, never with a lick and a promise."*

Just ask Alexander the Great. Over a drink.

Mint 27

TRUST
Given Not Earned
●

Today's EngageMINT
Give trust to others
with no strings attached.

U nexpectedly, the executive director showed up at the summer camp her organization sponsored. She made the rounds, inspected the facilities and noted the cracked window, the torn screen and the dirty walls. Then the executive confronted the camp director with the infractions. In a few hours the camp facilities were back in working order. Meanwhile on the other side of the lake, the executive director of another sponsoring organization showed up unexpectedly at their summer camp. She made no rounds. There was no inspection. She visited with the camp director and then together they walked randomly through the camp grounds and visited with other camp counselors without any predetermined itinerary or "rounds." The facilities were in good working order. No cracked windows. No torn screens. No dirty walls.

Why the difference? Trust. Trust given rather than earned. Trust given based on the leader's expectation of another rather than trust earned by the leader's inspection of another. "Trust is given not earned," state CEO Bob Chapman and co-author Raj Sisodia in their book *Everybody Matters*. To get good performance, leaders don't have to inspect it. They EXPECT it. Of course that flies in the face of the well-worn adage that management gets what management inspects. But inspection only nets compliance not a more empowering alliance. However, leaders with Great Expectations get even greater results—more than they expected and much more than they could ever inspect. With these Greater Expectations—with this focus on trusting another to perform well over time—there's an even greater sense of personal commitment, professional responsibility and continuous improvement. "Few things help an individual more than to place responsibility upon him (or her) and to let him (or her) know that you trust him," said noted author and educator Booker T. Washington. Grounded in that sense of responsibility, trust is the thrust of a quality-driven consistent performance. That kind of deep-seated and deep-seeded mutual trust develops OVER TIME. It's a mutual trust that is sown more than sewn—grown day—in and day—out over time—not something stitched together in time. It's a mutual trust sown like so many leadership seeds spawning growth and productivity. That's why the most effective leaders plant and fertilize these nine leadership behavioral seeds as defined by Stuart R. Levine and Michael A. Crom in their book *The Leader in You:*

> **Recognize people. Include them. Encourage them. Train them. Ask their opinions. Praise them. Let them make decisions. Give them the freedom to work as they see fit. And convey your belief in their abilities by getting out of the way.**

But most of all: trust them with no demand of reciprocal behavior. The most effective leaders realize they still have to EARN their trust from their constituents no matter how much they GIVE their trust to those same constituents. In earning trust from their employees, leaders do all nine of those behaviors listed above with integrity, humility and empathy. With integrity, leaders consistently do what they say. With humility, leaders admit their mistakes and give credit to others. With empathy, leaders share in the feelings, concerns and interests of others. And together, leaders and their employees, develop a culture of caring and sharing. Then they work out the kinks and squeaks in their relationship with a trust that is—according to leadership professor and author Warren Bennis—the "lubricant that makes it possible for organizations to work," Without an inspection.

Mint 28

Parlay Your
PYGMALION POWER

●

Today's EngageMINT
*Stimulate performance
with high expectations.*

Geneneral Douglas MacArthur took off his own Distinguished Service Cross the day before a planned battle in World War II and pinned it on his battalion commander. "I'm confident you will earn that Distinguished Service Cross when you lead your men into battle tomorrow," MacArthur predicted. Not if, when. He did. And they were victorious. Leaders "pre-ward" their followers.

What's a "pre-ward?" Same as a reward except a "pre-ward" is presented BEFORE an expected behavior or performance. A "pre-ward" galvanizes expectations and sparks enhanced performance. A "pre-ward" ups the ante in personal expectation to an act of faith in others that can turn the ordinary into the extraordinary. A "pre-ward" could be the teacher who calls her students "scholars" or the football coach who calls his players "student athletes." A "pre-ward" could be renaming a department in an organization to stimulate new behavior like the police chief who renamed his internal investigative unit the Internal Prevention Unit to focus more on ethics and standards in their investigations. The result was a 70 percent reduction in customer complaints.

A "pre-ward" could be re-titling a job description. Consider the patient who caught the hospital technician off guard with a "pre-ward" while he was routinely drawing a blood sample. The patient asked: "How long have you been a Care Giver?" The technician was surprised. No one had ever called him a Care Giver before. Nurses and doctors and social workers might use the term —Care Giver—to define themselves but not a medical technician, he thought. But then the technician broke out of the cold stone of his job function. He breathed a new sense of purpose. And he smiled at his newly perceived value he was bringing to others beyond a simple diagnostic test.

Do you have too many cold statues working for you? Then bring them back to life with your own act of faith in them. Parlay your Pygmalion Power. You'll recall, Pygmalion was a king who longed for companionship and love, according to Greek mythology. He was also a sculptor who created a statue of a beautiful woman. He loved that statue unconditionally. His dedication to the statue impressed Aphrodite so much that the Greek goddess of love brought the statue to life.

Likewise leaders can enlighten and empower their employees and figuratively bring them to life with their belief in them and in their abilities. The most effective leaders bring their employees to life with these Five Interaction Essentials created by Development Dimensions International (DDI), a leading leadership development organization:

1. Maintain or enhance self-esteem.
2. Listen and respond with empathy.
3. Ask for help, encourage involvement.
4. Share your thoughts and feelings.
5. Provide support.

Bring your team back to life. "Pre-ward" your team with an act of faith in them individually that enhances their self-esteem and your bottom line. "Pre-wards" can engender a sense of "responsible freedom" in the team member that is much more powerful than empowerment, according to Bob Chapman and Raj Sisodia in their book *Everybody Matters*. With "Pre-wards" leaders inspire others to be more reliant than merely compliant and to respond with more empathy than apathy.

Bringing Out The Best
IN OTHERS

●

Today's EngageMINT
*Rely on your insight as much as your sight
in assessing potential.*

F orlorn and frustrated, the prostitute stood mired in the mud of her past. So devastated, she convinced herself that she "was born in a pile of horse manure" and that she would "die in a pile of horse manure." Yet he saw something more enriching and ennobling in her eyes, something more promising in her future. To him, she was not a prostitute. She was: *The Sweet One.* She grimaced whenever he called her *The Sweet One*. She could never live up to that sweet expectation. No way, she protested. But he persisted. He was convinced she was *The Sweet One*. The more he persisted, the less she protested. And then slowly but steadily the more confident she became in living up to that Sweet One appellation and ensuing reputation.

At least that's the way it happened in the Broadway musical play and later in the movie: *The Man From La Mancha*. Dulcinea *(The Sweet One)* began doing works of compassion for others. The play ends with the former prostitute personally affirming her new identity: "My name is Dulcinea," she declares when someone calls her by her given name at birth, Aldonza. Dulcinea is more self-confident, more capable and more engaged in boosting the bottom-line.

As "Ken Blanchard and Spencer Johnson observe in their book *The New One-Minute Manager,* "People who feel good about themselves produce good results." To become an even more effective leader, how do you channel Don Quixote and express that kind of act of faith in your Dulcineas? How do you engineer a deep-seated trust in others that can transform behavior and renew a tattered reputation? How do you anoint key individuals on your team with meaningful characterizations that positively impact their performance and your bottom line? How do you cultivate the hidden Dulcinea's on your team—those team members known only superficially and often for something less than perfect performance in their past? Here's how: First take your time. Study your team carefully over time. And when you study them, take a lesson from Johnny Depp's lead character in the movie *Don Juan DeMarco:* Don't be LIMITED by your eyesight. Look at individuals on your team more strategically than ever before with an intuitive sense that goes deeper than assessing their past performance. Look more astutely with your heart and soul into the future than merely with your eyes into the past. And rely more on your insight than on your sight.

The Beauty Within

Search out what Don Juan DeMarco calls the "beauty" within." In the movie, Depp's character tells his psychiatrist—played by Marlon Brando— that his alluring influence over women stems from their "sense that I search out their beauty that is within them until it overwhelms everything else. And then they cannot avoid that desire to release that beauty and envelop me in it." Forget the sexual overtones or the Hollywood hype and sexist script that only an actor like Depp could get away with in the movies.

The key point is to focus on POSITIVE behaviors. Look for the possibilities—the potential —in a team member whose performance levels have fallen. Rely on your insight more than on your sight and search "for the beauty within" as Don Juan DeMarco asserts. Think of leadership as more than an act of faith in others. Think of your role as a leader as an act of love where you bring out the best in others no matter how high the baggage of life is piled or how deep the proverbial manure.

Mint 30

Give 'em
The VIP Treatment

●

Today's EngageMINT
*Preserve the dignity of others
in the face of conflict.*

Enthusiastically, the retail clerk raced into work and eagerly took charge of his cash register. He couldn't wait to start serving his customers with a personal banter that turned the tedious jobs of both the shopper and the cashier into a duet, a playful partnership of you-buy-I bag-and-we-smile together. He was good at what he did and everyone around him—his bosses, his peers, and his customers—knew it. Business was slow on this early Sunday morning. His cash register would remain silent at least for now. Neither his magic wand—the scanning device—nor his magnetic smile would be dazzling anyone right now.

With no customers in sight, he began sweeping and cleaning his cashier's station. But soon he got bored. He needed something more creative, more productive, and more meaningful to do. His manager knew just what to do to engage his star performer. He assigned him to serve as a greeter at the main entrance where the consummate people person would have a chance to interact with everyone who came into the store. But the twinkle in the eyes of the star performer faded again. He got bored. Again. Indeed, he was a roll-your-up-sleeves-and-get-busy type retail clerk.

Finally the boredom overwhelmed him. Frustrated, he reached into the large pocket of his store-issued vest and pulled out a small pocket-book that he read during breaks and lunch. "Ah, at last I have something to do," he said to himself, as he stood guard at the entrance while reading his book. His manager saw that book's red cover from a distance and like an enraged bull charged at the retail clerk from what seemed halfway across the store. "You can't be reading a book on the

job like that!" The stunned employee fired back with equal venom: "Yes I can!" Then he boomed even louder in an uncharacteristic bombastic tone. "Oh, yes I can!" "No, no, no...." the manager retorted, walking away in utter disgust. The manager was on the verge of firing an employee whose star had always burned brightly as an ideal employee. And now the star performer was on the verge of quitting or being fired. The manager, so furious with the flagrant book reader on company time, ordered his one-time best employee to get out of his sight: "Go face (straighten) the soup cans (on the shelf)."

The seething employee bolted out of his greeter's role, eager to be doing something—anything—other than just standing around aimlessly and staring blankly into the isolation of the store on this raw morning. The manager and the employee hardly spoke the rest of the day even as customer traffic increased and the cashier resumed his mastery over the scanning wand. But the magic was gone. The employee worked with less vigor for the rest of the day. The flare-up hurt. The business lost the full services of a high-performing employee. The manager lost any rapport he had earned with the employee. And the star employee felt de-valued — as if his more than 14-months of previous stellar service counted for nothing. He felt humiliated, scorned and disrespected. He took his frustration out on the company's bottom-line with less productivity and little or no value-added customer service or creative problem-solving.

The VIP Treatment

There has to be a better way of correcting the behavior of good employees who do bad things. Let's face it: reading a book while you are on the job as a greeter of customers isn't exactly staying customer focused. The star employee was definitely wrong. Could it be the manager was also wrong? What would a leader have done that the manager didn't? How would a loving leader go about reining in the employee without raining on the employee's parade of previous high performance? A loving leader would give the offending employee the V-I-P treatment. In this case, V-I-P is a three-step process that turns an ordinary "Fire 'em" solution into an extraordinary "Fire 'em up" resolution. Energized leaders and engaged employees think of V-I-P as a three-step process of Validating, Identifying, and Preserving engaged, creative and productive employees regardless of changing work environment conditions:

In VALIDATING:

The Loving Leader first acknowledges the star performer's reputation for productive and creative work.

In IDENTIFYING:

The Loving Leader assesses the situation and defines the CURRENT value of an employee's skill sets that have contributed to his or her reputation for productive behavior.

In PRESERVING:

The Loving Leader reminds the employee of his or her stellar reputation and provides him or her a face-saving way to preserve the integrity of that previous performance especially when the working conditions change (such as a slow day in the store) or conflict ensues.

Study the following VIP Treatment as it would be applied to this situation where a high performing employee is reading a book while serving as the greeter at the door of a retail store. His team leader approaches the employee and says:

VALIDATING

"Joe, you always are highly productive and even now when it's slow you find a way to stay busy reading. I think of you as the ultimate multi-tasker. I wonder though if you could be tarnishing your reputation for the way you always anticipate the needs of our customers if you aren't able to gain immediate eye contact as they enter the store.

IDENTIFYING

"I know it's boring standing here when few

customers come through the door. But I like to think of myself as the captain of the ship when I have door duty. I am welcoming people on board this ship. And I am not sure my customers coming on board would think the best of me as their captain if I wasn't focused more on them than on my reading.

PRESERVING

"Joe you are the captain of this ship right now in your greeter's role and your passengers — your customers—need what you give them so creatively, so productively day in and day out at your register just as much here at the door: your undivided attention. You've always been a great example to the other employees as a top performer. It will get busier soon and then you will be going back to your cash register. But right now, Captain, we need you to read the eyes of our customers like you do so well and save the reading of those pages in that book for later."

Joe shoved the book back in his pocket and smiled proudly at the leader's hopeful tone. Suddenly he felt enriched. He was paid more than money could buy. He was paid respect. Soon the store got busier and Joe returned to his first love—cashiering—with even more energy, enthusiasm and magic in his wand. He had been Validated. His work Identified. And his reputation Preserved. Joe had been treated much more personally and professionally in way that both enriched and celebrated his talents beyond his status as a VIP, a Very Important Person. He earned the VIP Treatment from a loving leader who sought to care— by design— rather than from a manager who sought to control— by default.

Mint 31

VALUING OTHERS
To Boost the Bottom Line

Today's EngageMINT
*Caring not controlling
heightens human performance.*

Vandalism costs at the county jail fell by 80 percent the year after the new Sheriff came to town. His secret? Perks. The Sheriff awarded more perks to inmates who were charged with lesser crimes. He treated them as citizens of his community more than as denizens of the local lockup. He treated them as people with feelings not simply inmates with records. And he treated them with a keen deference to their circumstances not a routine indifference to their situation. The Sheriff gave one bald inmate a baseball cap to help him keep warm. He allowed another to work part time in the county's garage. And he gave more regular smoking breaks to others.

The net result? Vandalism by disgruntled inmates decreased so much that maintenance costs that year were only 20 percent of the previous year. Why? A nurturing leader, according to David Kelley, the founder of the leading industrial design firm, IDEO. Kelley says "If we were to measure what makes a leader here it would be to measure how nurturing people are." Nurturing leaders know the power in treating others the way you would want to be treated. Nurturing leaders embrace the virtuous leadership sentiments of Confucius who said: "If you use laws to direct people and punishments to control them, they will only evade the laws and develop no conscience. But if you guide them by virtue and control them by customs, they will have a conscience and a sense of what is right."

Maybe that's why Diligent Dick had perfect attendance for 41 years as a production worker at a global furniture maker. Not even a bloody hand injury and 18 stitches OFF the job could keep Diligent Dick from showing up to work on time just 10 hours later. So what if 17-inches of snow fell in one 30-hour period? Diligent Dick would get up at 2:30 am to shovel his driveway and still get to work on time by 5:30 am. He felt a personal connection to his bosses and peers at Steelcase Inc. He felt valued and appreciated. He was motivated by virtue and custom not rules and regulations at his company. With respect comes enhanced performance. In fact respect and mutual trust are "arguably the most important part" of Walt Disney's definition of leadership according to the authors of *The Disney Way,* Bill Capodagli and Lynn Jackson. They say respect and mutual trust represent a common thread of best-practice companies that masterfully applied Walt Disney's "definition of leadership* to grow and nurture their cultures."

That's why loving leaders respect their employees, nourish their talents and nurture their potential. General Dwight Eisenhower nurtured the potential of the common soldier, saying: "In our army, every private had at least a second lieutenant's gold bars somewhere in him and he was helped and encouraged to earn them." Napoleon also encouraged and nurtured the common soldier. He paid particular respect to a soldier whose horse dropped dead from exhaustion just after the soldier delivered a critical message to Napoleon. "Here take my horse," Napoleon said. The soldier balked. "Your horse is too good for me, a common soldier." Napoleon scoffed: "Nothing is too good or too magnificent for a common soldier." Napoleon knew that paying another respect can be even more enriching in boosting the bottom line more profitably. Even with nothing more than the warmth of a baseball cap or the comfort of a smoke break.

> **Leadership is "the ability to establish and manage a creative climate in which individuals and teams are self-motivated to successful achievement of long term goals in an environment of mutual trust and respect."*
> **--Walt Disney**

Mint 32

Mustering Your Courage To
FACE YOURSELF

Today's EngageMINT
Discover who you are inside
to better interact with others outside.

He was a self-described jerk. He had little time or patience for others. He was always too busy, too stressed and too depressed. And to make matters worse as a stone mason he knew how to launch a rock or two when he needed to blow off some steam. Today, Mark Fernandes is the Chief Leadership Officer at Luck Companies, one of the nation's largest family-owned construction aggregate companies in Richmond, VA. How do you transform yourself from a self-described jerk into a values-based leader? With courage, the courage to look into the mirror. "We all had to find out who we were on the inside, how we show up on the outside (personality style and behaviors) and what impact we were having around others," Fernandes recalled. "I had to learn to look in the mirror not out of the windshield and man that is hard."

Growth had overwhelmed the company's management structure. New hires exacerbated the contentious business climate while snarky executives rattled their sabers in a plethora of meetings-after-the-meeting. And talented employees like Mark Fernandes seethed in the storm until one day he took matters into his own hands –and fist– and punched a hole into an office wall. Later that day, the CEO — Charles Luck IV —stepped in with a sense of humor and a loving leader's mindset. He flashed a smile of caring rather than a stern look of disdain. "First of all stop breaking all my stuff around here," the CEO laughed. Then citing the 10-year history of Fernandes as a significant contributor to the company, the CEO decided to focus their collective frustration into something more productive. "Okay you want to change things around here and so do I. So let's work on this together." The CEO then set up a series of meetings with a leadership development firm. He asked Fernandes to be the point man for those meetings and determine how Luck Companies could develop its management team to better cope with the company's growth.

Fernandes discovered that Luck Companies needed leaders who could move in step WITH others not step OVER others. But Fernandes noted that many would-be leaders—including himself —were reluctant to dance to the new music that no longer tuned in solely to your position on an organizational chart or your access to a budget account. Now leaders had to listen to each other and collaborate with each other before they collectively could hear the new music and then progressively dance their way in harmony together to a more profitable, more productive and more personally engaging company.

Today employees are aligned around key values and beliefs that drive the mission of the company to "ignite human potential through Values Based Leadership." That focus on supporting employees with something more than a paycheck began when the company founder would cook lunch for his then 14 employees every day at the worksite in the late 1920s and early 1930s. Charles Luck Jr. purchased an old railroad dining car and had it situated near the quarry where his modern-day Fred Flintstones carved out rocks and crushed stone, sand and gravel. The founder's son fostered that same pay-it-forward, caring and sharing philosophy when he became the Chief Executive Officer more than three decades ago. He even placed signage in key areas throughout the company proclaiming "We Care." Today as loving leaders they care enough to look at themselves in the mirror every day and ask: "Who are we on the inside and how are we acting on the outside to enhance the potential in others?"

Mint 33

INTERPRETING
The 5 Languages of Love

Today's EngageMINT
*Appreciate others
the way they prefer.*

Archie Bunker, the head of the household in that socially pioneering TV sitcom of yesteryear *All in the Family*, was always right. In his mind. And everyone else around him was just wrong especially when he spoke Ex Cathedra (from his chair in his fabled living room in Queens, NY). Even the Pope might have laughed at Archie's sense of his infallibility. In one episode, Archie says. "Edith do you know why I can't communicate? Because I'm talking in English and you're listening in dingbat!" Not exactly. Archie's personal conviction was too self-centered to be effective, too righteous to be right. As every leader knows, in order to engage others, in order to get them to pay attention to you, you first have to pay attention to them.

That's why loving leaders adapt their communications style to the individual preferences of their listeners/ followers. And that's why loving leaders also learn to adapt their behavior and wrap their convictions with a ribbon that would most appeal PERSONALLY to each of their direct reports. "The object of love is not getting something you want but doing something for the well-being of the one you love," according to Gary Chapman, author of *The Five Love Languages.* That means leaders treat others the way they want to be treated. And that's why loving leaders learn to "speak" the love language that each of their direct reports prefers. Consider these Five Love Languages that Chapman cites:

1. *Words of Affirmation* (compliments)
2. *Quality Time* (mentoring etc.)
3. *Receiving Gifts* (tickets to the theater etc.)
4. *Acts of Service* (a ride to the airport etc.)

5. *Physical Touch* (a hand shake, a pat on the back etc.).

Your direct reports have different needs but the same objective. They all want to be appreciated on their terms. And the most effective way to appreciate someone is to speak their language more personally and to listen to their needs more intently. No wonder that psychologist William James, said "possibly the deepest human need is the need to feel appreciated." On their terms. That's why the most effective leaders adapt and adjust to others as noted in the first book in *The Leadership Mints Series*, **THINKING Like a Leader** by Peter Jeff, (Mint 58):

"The most effective leaders think of themselves as if they are heading a bevy of birds as different at Eagles, Peacocks, Doves and Owls. Leaders must adapt to the needs of each of those different birds so they all will perch on the same branch at the same time. To earn that alignment, the most effective leaders first define each bird's chief need:

- *EAGLES celebrate proven results.*
- *PEACOCKS relish personal anecdotes.*
- *DOVES require conformity.*
- *OWLS seek documentation.*

How do leaders discern the differences in their birds that comprise their teams? They observe their different behaviors in routine matters: EAGLES (cholerics) take charge. PEACOCKS (sanguines) are the life of the party. DOVES (phlegmatics) are calm and composed. OWLS (melancholics) are methodical and serious. Each of the birds on your team may sing a different song but it is the effective leader who parlays their team's individual strengths and complements their individual singing to align in harmony. Then you will have these birds of a different feather eating right out of your hand."

Especially if you are speaking their language of love. Personally. And professionally.

ENTITLEMENTS
Resisting the Temptation

●

Today's EngageMINT
Show more than tell.
Actions speak louder than words.

B ound for the airport, the CEO and the president of a multi-billion dollar company headed off on a business trip. No limousine. No private jet. No first class treatment. They flew commercial—in coach. Of course, the CEO and President could have justified the expense in deploying one of their jets in their corporate fleet for a business trip. But on this occasion, they had planned a larger than normal window in their schedules to accommodate the added travel time. And they saved a lot more than money.

They reinforced an egalitarian working environment between management and employees as partners in production and in profits. Their frugal behavior in effect sent a clear message to all employees in the privately-held, profit-sharing company—let's work together as efficiently as we can with as little waste as possible.

Yet the temptation is often too great, especially for middle managers who see their peers at other companies getting the first class treatment. They may feel under so much stress they can easily justify padding their expense account a few hundred dollars more for their share of the first class treatment. However that short-term convenience can quickly stretch into an expectation that over time becomes an arrogant entitlement that contaminates a loving culture of caring and sharing.

Consider the two middle managers on a business trip who returned to the corporate hangar following their day-long meetings. They were told their company's jet had three open seats for their flight back to corporate headquarters. They could save the company the cost of the commercial plane tickets they held that same evening. However the company jet wasn't going to take off for another three hours. The two middle managers conferred and realized that if they flew commercial they could get back "in time tonight to watch (a favorite television show)" before DVRs and On Demand programming. They chose to spend the added flight expense on THEMSELVES. And they failed to teach the newly hired supervisor flying with them a critical lesson in the culture of the company: Think We Not Me!

Think We Not Me!

The most effective leaders know only too well that they are always on stage—in the spotlight —at least as far as their employees and other constituents are concerned. The most effective leaders never under-estimate the power they have to influence behavior with their own personal example. Take it from Sam Walton, the founder of Walmart, writing in his autobiography *Sam Walton, Made in America* on the significance of leading by example:

> *"A lot of people think it's crazy of me to fly coach whenever I go on a commercial flight, and maybe I do overdo it a bit. But I feel like it's up to me as a leader to set an example.*
>
> *"It's not fair for me to ride one way and ask everybody else to ride another way. The minute you do that, you start building resentment and your whole team idea begins to strain at the seams."*

Indeed, the best leaders coach. In coach.

Speak Softly &
Carry A Big Schtick
●

Today's EngageMINT
*Maintain self-esteem
in resolving conflict.*

Can you argue without being argumentative? Can you command without being commanding? Can you rule without ruling? Can you dictate without dictating? Loving leaders can. In reprimanding others to enhance overall performance, the most effective leaders have learned to speak softly and carry a big Schtick. They speak with a well-thought out Schtick —a process or routine — as the dictionary defines "Schtick." You too can carry a big Schtick. The key is to prepare your reprimand from the employee's point of view. Ask yourself this critical question: how will he or she feel if you simply order something to be done rather than put things in order to let them get done? That's the leadership difference. Next time you're planning to reprimand someone or persuade them to change their behavior, appeal to the offending person's ego.

Consider this example of speaking softly and carrying a big Schtick from former General Colin Powell. In his book *It Worked For Me,* Powell recalled how one Marine Commandant gained support for an unpopular decision: banning swagger sticks. Ego was clearly at play here. Powell explained that soldiers brandished the swagger sticks more as an arrogant show of their personal power rather than as a tool of their military might. The Marine Commandant knew it would be counter-productive for him to simply issue a command: Stop carrying the swagger sticks. So he issued a memo reaffirming his permission to use the swagger sticks albeit with a Schtick attached: "Officers are authorized to carry swagger sticks if they feel the need." Of course no self-respecting marine "felt the need" to augment their personal fighting street cred and in time fewer and fewer marines wore the swagger sticks. With a Schtick, the most effective leaders sell more than tell and earn greater buy-in from their followers in changing behavior without losing face and without feeling threatened. Consider the following example:

Four veteran supervisors in your manufacturing plant are taking their smoke breaks in the entrance to the building in violation of the company policy. Over the next two weeks, you notice more employees and those same supervisors in that plant taking their smoke breaks in the same entry way at least 100 feet from the designated smoking area. Finally as the company president you can't stand it anymore. Your supervisors are setting a bad example. You see your company health insurance rates going up again. You know you have to reprimand these supervisors. But then you balk. You fault yourself for looking the other way too long after the smoking policy was issued. You know only too well these same veteran manufacturing supervisors have made you rich over the last 20 years. They've driven your bottom line to the bank time and time again. Now what do you do?

Consider unveiling your <u>Schtick</u> with personality and poise like this: The company president greeted the supervisors smoking in the entry way. He offered them each a cigar that he said was from his personal collection. Then he said very sincerely, "I sure hope you guys enjoy that cigar and do me a favor: enjoy it over there (he pointed to company's designated smoking area). They say the smokes taste a lot better there."

Selling more than telling.

The <u>Schtick</u> worked. The supervisors started smoking in the designated area. In time, the other employees who enjoyed smoke breaks followed the example of the supervisors and reaffirmed a key leadership skill that Deborah Tannen writes about in her book *The Argument Culture:* "All human relations require us to find ways to get what we want from others without seeming to dominate them. Allowing others to feel you are doing what they want for a reason less humiliating to them fills this need." No wonder loving leaders speak softly and carry a big-Schtick.

Mint 36

Making Commitments With Your
Due-To List
●

-Today's EngageMINT
*Focus first on your strategic purpose
before making commitments.*

Running from one meeting to the next, the vice president was late. Again. He rationalized his tardiness on the importance of his position: "I have too much responsibility to parcel my time out to the precise minute," he would tell himself. "Besides I can be a few minutes late. The important aspects of the meeting usually don't start until a few minutes into the meeting anyway." But that was before he met the new company president. The vice president was always was on time for her meetings.

One day the president seemed to be in a philosophical mood when she met with this vice president for their regular one-on-one. She mentioned that she was reading a book on George Washington. She said that as president he would often invite new members of Congress for dinner and sometimes his guests would arrive a few minutes late. They were embarrassed to find the president eating even if none of the guests had arrived on time. She noted that Washington said that his "cook never asks if the visitors have arrived but if the hour has arrived." Dinner was always served at 4 pm. Promptly.

The new company president noted that Washington showed respect for the timely performance of his cook rather than pay a courtesy to his late arriving guests. Then the new company president seized her teaching moment. She looked at her calendar for the day. "So much to do and so little time," the new company president said to the vice president. "But as a leader I know I have to invest my time. Not spend it. Invest it on making commitments not spend in on making appointments. I keep telling myself anyone can make appointments but it takes a leader to make commitments they keep." Ever since then, the vice president's punctuality at other meetings improved. He showed more reverence for making a commitment to someONE rather than an appointment to someTHING. He came to understand that it was more important to fulfill his commitments with attention rather than to fill his calendar full with intention.

Consider the president of a billion-dollar plus world leading company who accepted an invitation to attend an annual awards luncheon hosted by his company's Toastmasters Club — a voluntary organization open to all employees who commit themselves to learning and practicing public speaking, active listening and leadership development once a week on their own time. However, the morning of the Toastmasters Award Luncheon the company was notified that it was being sued by a competitor for patent infringement. The legal department was bristling. So were teams of engineers reviewing the particulars of the legal suit. The president was in closed-door meetings all morning. But at 12 noon, the president showed up at the Toastmasters Awards Luncheon. On time. The leader of the company's Toastmasters club was stunned. She thought for sure the company president would be buried in all things legal.

Focus First on Your Due-To List

Later that day, the leader of the Toastmasters Club found the CEO in his office about 6 pm and thanked him again for attending the Toastmasters luncheon. She said she knew how busy he must have been with the law suit and that she really didn't think he'd make the meeting. "I made a commitment to you," the president deadpanned. End of story. That's what the most effective leaders do. They make commitments more than appointments. Their commitments are anchored in a "due-to" list more than a to-do list.

The most effective leaders realize you commit first to a DUE To list long before you develop a To Do list. A DUE TO list is comprised of long-range commitments that bring goals into a clearer, more realistic focus based on well-defined values. Like a train, effective goal-setting is a process of linking not listing— linking a list of things To Do to a clearer rationale that is DUE TO a higher purpose, a conviction, a value such as punctuality out of respect for others. Maybe that's why Mahatma Gandhi always wore a watch—albeit a cheap $1 pocket watch—on a string around his waist. Significantly, the famed civil rights leader in India often wore a loin cloth and not much more other than his watch in fulfilling his vow of simplicity.

Gandhi, like the most effective leaders, knew that punctuality reinforces your sense of commitment to others and your stewardship of your most precious resource: time. The most effective leaders realize that time is their most fleeting resource. No matter how rich you are. Even the most resourceful leaders can't manufacture an antique, print a masterpiece, or bottle a vintage wine. It takes time.

Investing Not Spending Your Time

So precious is TIME that Queen Elizabeth said she would give all her possessions for just a MOMENT of it. And the Great Magi in Voltaire's book *Zadig* says that time is: "the most regretted, without which nothing can be done which devours all that is little and enlivens all that is great."

Maybe that's why historians tell us that some leaders celebrated TIME like Marie Antoinette, the last Queen of France who received 51 watches to mark her engagement. Some avidly tracked time like inventor Buckminster Fuller who always wore three watches when he traveled: one set to current time, one set to his home office time and one set to his destination time. Others tried to manipulate time like the quick-thinking Army captain did in 1889 for the inauguration of President–elect Benjamin Harrison. Extending a long pole, he pushed back the hands of the clock at the Capitol so that the president would be on-time for his inauguration.

Still others seek to extend time the way Ulysses implored the mythological god Athena to extend the night so that he could have even more time to make love to his wife on his first night home after 20 years at war and lost at sea. But at the end of the day the most effective leaders leverage the incessant passage and power of time to better focus on the present, to better seize the day to fulfill their commitments. Carpe Diem! That's why the most effective leaders pay homage to the always-flowing, ever-changing currents of time that prisoners serve, musicians mark and historians record. No one has more of it. All of us have all of it. And yet, we are always running out of it. Leaders are ever mindful of the the temporal but ever-accelerating significance of time as depicted in the following poem by Henry Twells—amended by Guy Pentreath—and showcased at the *TIME Exhibit* at the Museum of Science and Industry in Chicago:

> *"For when I was a babe and wept.*
> *And slept. Time crept.*
> *When I was a boy and*
> *laughed. And talked. Time walked.*
> *Then when I was a man.*
> *Time ran.*
> *But as I got older and grew,*
> *Time flew."*

Time flies so quickly. That's why loving leaders consider time so precious they start each day as if they had just found a Time Treasure Chest filled with $86,400. That's how much money you would have if you had one dollar for every second in a 24-hour day. The most effective leaders fiercely guard and shrewdly invest in that Time Treasure Chest.

In summary, the most effective leaders don't merely spend time with others by appointment. They invest time in others with a commitment. As investors not speculators, they know that leadership is a "conscious commitment" not a title or a role observes Bob Chapman, the CEO of Barry Wehmiller, the $2 billion manufacturing technology conglomerate with more than 11,000 employees. And loving leaders in particular invest their time beyond a to-do list with a due-to list rooted in a well-defined purpose that ultimately saves time.

Dare To Be Humble!

●

Today's EngageMINT
*Humility fortifies strength
in tense situations.*

General Colin Powell, then the nation's top military officer, kept a special phone line in his office that only he would answer. He gave the phone number to people he trusted to keep his ego in check; to make sure he was staying connected to the real world and to make sure he knew when he was naked wearing the Emperor's Clothes. All leaders have their version of a Hotline to act quickly to divert a crisis, but how many leaders like General Powell have a PERSONAL Hotline — let's call it —a *SNOTLINE*—to help them avert a personal crisis? How many leaders would ask their friends to critique their behavior and alert them to what they can't see for themselves—like the proverbial snot hanging from their noses? Installing that *SNOTLINE* took humility, discipline and emotional intelligence. With that deeply-developed sense of humility a leader develops an even more personal connection to his own narrative, to his own understanding of himself and others that helps a leader be even more real and therefore even more credible and potent as a leader.

Leaders dare to be humble. As Norman Vincent Peale and Ken Blanchard echoed: "People with humility don't think less of themselves. They just think about themselves less." And therefore humble leaders have more time and energy to "invest in others," as author Tony Schwartz writes in his book *The Way We're Working Isn't Working*. "Genuine humility frees us of the need to protect an image of ourselves or stand above others. (Humility) gives us permission instead to accept, embrace and learn." How can you become more humble with greater wisdom and character in real-life situations? Let's scan the history books for real-world examples of leaders who dared to be humble: Booker T. Washington, the author and educator, was walking along 42nd Street in New York carrying a heavy suitcase. A stranger offered to help him carry the suitcase. They walked together and chatted. "And that was the first time I ever saw Theodore Roosevelt," Washington recalled years later. Leaders dare to be humble.

Consider the man who stood in the lobby as a capacity crowd streamed into the concert hall to hear the famous pianist. An attendant thought the man had not seen the "sold-out" sign and said: "I am sorry we have no available seats." The man nodded politely and said quietly: "May I be seated at the piano?" The man was famed pianist Arthur Rubenstein—the main attraction that evening. Leaders dare to be humble. Maybe that's why the most effective and loving leaders leverage their sense of humility as a teaching tool.

Consider this scenario: An elderly lady came on board a train. She was carrying a large basket. There were no vacant seats. She finally reached the back of the train. The man in the last seat on the train rose promptly and gave the lady his seat. Immediately 20 men were on their feet offering the man his seat. "No gentlemen, if there was no seat for this old lady there is no seat for me." The man was General Robert E. Lee. Leaders dare to be humble.

And finally consider this scenario when a man on a train lit a cigar. The lady sitting behind him chided the man: "You are probably a foreigner and do not know that there is a smoking-car attached to the train. Smoking is not permitted here." The man quietly threw away his cigar. Later the conductor told the woman that she had mistakenly entered the private car of General Ulysses S. Grant. Leaders dare to be humble. As Leonard Sweet observes in his book *Summoned to Lead:* "When leaders are called forth they don't so much rise to the occasion as bow to the invitation." With humility.

Mint 38

Hey Pops,
Where's Coffee?
●

Today's EngageMINT
Respect others regardless
of their status.

Hoping this was the job interview he had been trying to land, the young executive couldn't wait to meet the CEO of a prominent company in their industry. The two met in the lobby of a hotel hosting their industry's annual convention. Then they ventured to find a restaurant in the hotel for their breakfast meeting. As they turned a corner, the CEO saw an elderly gentleman waiting patiently for the elevator. "Hey Pops, where's coffee?" the CEO blurted. The elegantly dressed man lifted his cane to indicate the direction of the restaurant. Instantly, the young executive lost his appetite for the job and for breakfast.

The young executive thought to himself: "If my potential boss treats a stranger that dismissively how will he treat one of his direct reports?" Such boorish behavior often leads to a self-serving attitude, an escalating arrogance and a heightened self-importance that diminishes the dignity and the self-worth of others. You can judge the character of a person by how well they treat those "who can do nothing for them," according to German philosopher Johann Wolfgang Goethe. That's why loving leaders treat everyone with respect no matter if they sweep their floors, park their cars or pour their coffee.

"Watch out for people who have a situational value system, who can turn the charm on and off depending on the status of the person they are interacting with," observed Bill Swanson, then CEO at Raytheon who wrote a booklet titled *33 Unwritten Rules of Management.* One of those 33 rules is: "A person who is nice to you but rude to the waiter, or to others, is not a nice person." Putting down others in order to put yourself up on pedestal undermines individual dignity and worth. It undermines learning from each other and it diminishes the diversity that thwarts more authentic decision making. That's why the most effective leaders do much more than simply react instinctively and defensively. They respond thoughtfully and empathetically, often with a sense of humor even in the most embarrassing situations for the people they're interacting with.

Consider the scenario when two executives were having dinner at an upscale restaurant to discuss strategy for an upcoming negotiating session. Their busy server accidentally spilled a glass of red wine on one of the executives. How would you have reacted? This executive simply smiled at the flustered and contrite server and joked that the wine stains almost matched his red tie. Meanwhile the other executive filed the accidental wine spill in his memory banks under poise in facing a fast-changing situation. Later that week, the more senior executive asked his wine-stained partner to take the lead in their stalled negotiations even though he had less experience. Somehow the more experienced executive already knew that his partner had the poise and composure to turn the whine of a negotiation into the wine of a celebration.

How can you best prepare your staff (future leaders) to be that empathetic and self-effacing? Introduce them to your company's janitors or maintenance people and point out the value-add services they bring to the company. Take a cue from leaders at West Point Academy in launching your Know-Your-Janitor initiative. Ask a provocative question on a written exam: "Name two maintenance people who work in this building? Many students balked, saying this last question on a written examination for a course in military leadership was not relevant. But the professor—an Army captain stood firm—according to Scott Snair in his book *West Point Leadership Lessons*. Treating everyone with respect is a leadership requisite regardless of their status. No matter if they are wielding a cane or a wine glass.

Get Off Your Buts!

●

Today's EngageMINT:
*Leverage conflict
to enhance performance.*

D r. McCoy and Mr. Spock are reunited on the starship for the first time in years in *Star Trek The Motion Picture*. McCoy—the affable people-oriented physician—sniffs at Spock—the cold, aloof, analytical half human science officer: "You are as warm as ever and you haven't changed." And Spock, his voice dripping with equal sarcasm, retorts: "Nor have you changed, doctor, as your continued predilection for irrelevancy demonstrates."

Friction is the natural by-product when obstinate personalities clash. But without friction there would be no real power. Everything would quite literally slip away. So the most effective leaders do more than simply grease the points of friction in their organizations. They leverage it. They recognize feuding like that between McCoy and Spock—born in personality differences and bred in high-stress work environments—is bound to happen in any organization whenever and wherever highly intelligent, ambitious, opinionated people come together.

And leaders know it is more productive to deal with— more than duel with—those scoundrels who brighten the room every time they leave it, those scoundrels who smack of incite more than insight. No wonder the most effective leaders agree with the wit who said: "It's not the ups and downs of life that bother me. It's the jerks." Loving leaders learn how to deal with those jerks. They weave together torn and tattered feelings into a quilt of understanding sewn with a degree of respect for each other's point of view. They know that it is too easy to find the negative in any situation, too easy to find a flaw and too easy to change the tone of discussion from upbeat to beat-up. Leaders conquer conflict with something more than the standard "Yes….but" mantra. Leaders get off their "buts" like this:

Instead of "BUT-ting" in and defending their point of view with a phrase that rolls off their tongue virtually at will: "Yes, but…"They respond: "Yes, **AND**."

Instead of "BUT-ting" in and challenging others directly: "But, what it really means is," they say diplomatically: "**AND**, it could also mean."

Instead of "BUT-ting" in and flatly rejecting another's opinion with a blunt outburst: "You're wrong," they say— "You're probably right, from your point of view. **AND** there might be another way to look at this that would also make sense to both of us."

Instead of "BUT-ting" in-and defending yourself with a phrase like "You don't understand" the most energized leaders and engaged employees take the sting out of that charge by saying, "**AND** help me to better understand your concerns."

Conflict:
The Gadfly of Thought

The most effective leaders see conflict as "the gadfly of thought," as John Dewey, the education reformer, noted. Dewey could have been speaking of loving leaders when he added: "Conflict is a sine qua non of reflection and ingenuity. It stirs us to observation and memory. It instigates invention. It shocks us out of sheep-like passivity." That's why loving leaders realize that conflict can serve as a catalyst for more viable relationships as long as they can start anew and stay open to new points of view. Make no 'buts' —about it.

Mint 40

Becoming the
Monkey in the Middle

●

Today's EngageMINT
Beware how others see you.

Remember playing Monkey-in-the-Middle as a kid? Now you're a CEO (or a department head or team leader) and you know only too well that you are still the Monkey-in-the-Middle. No wonder "being a boss is much like being a higher status primate in any group, the creatures beneath you in the pecking order watch every move you make and so they know a lot more about you than you know about them," observes Robert Sutton writing in his book *Good Boss, Bad Boss.*

All eyes are on you no matter where you are or how high you climb. Even the most insular leaders soon realize there is always someone above you (the board of directors, stockholders, government regulators etc.) looking down on you and so many more below you looking up to you from a reference point you never see. As the CEO, you happen to be the monkey in the highest seat in the tree. From your perch, you can look down and see other smiling monkeys but when they look up to you they see anything "butt" smiling faces. And from that perspective they can only assume the organization stinks, according to Captain D. Michael Abrashoff, writing in his book *It's Your Ship.*

That's why "the key to being a successful skipper is to see the ship through the eyes of the crew," And the best way to do that is to play your role as The Monkey in the Middle. That's why the most effective leaders work hard to see things from their employees' point of view no matter how high they sit in the organization or even how high they have orbited around the world. Astronaut John Glenn found that out: perspective is always in the eye of the beholder. The first man to orbit the earth in 1962, Glenn earned worldwide fame. Everybody it seemed looked up to him—everyone that is except Caroline, the four-year-old daughter of President John Kennedy. Her mom introduced her to Glenn a few days after he splashed down from orbiting the earth at 17,000 miles an hour. "This is the astronaut who went around the earth in the spaceship," her mom, Jacqueline Kennedy proudly proclaimed. Caroline smiled and then seemed perplexed, as Glenn recalled in his memoirs:

> *"Caroline looked at me*
> *and then all around and then she*
> *turned back to me.*
> *"Her face disappointed and*
> *she said in a quavering voice,*
> *"But where's the monkey?"*

The four-year-old reacted normally to the facts presented to her: astronaut + spaceship = monkey. That was her frame of reference when it came to outer space, rocket ships, and orbiting the earth. The monkey was literally in the middle of everyone's attention. At least that's what Caroline recalled seeing on the black and white television screens. During her lifetime up to then, 30 monkeys were groomed for space flight including a rhesus monkey named Able and a squirrel monkey named Miss Baker. They became the first monkeys to return to earth after space flight. So it was only logical at least from a four-year old's point of view to raise a concern about the absent monkeys when only a human being returned to earth safe and sound.

No wonder the most loving leaders pay homage to the power of perception. They know understanding the point of view of others is key to making a vital connection. Especially when you're the monkey in the middle of it all.

Mint 41

Kneading Yourself
Back to Life

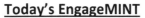

Today's EngageMINT
Express your need
for human interaction.

ang. Bang. Bang. The pounding in the kitchen gets louder and louder and LOUDER! The vice president is home working in his kitchen—with a rolling-pin. He is pounding, pushing and pulling the dough into delicious bread. Of course, it would be so much easier and more efficient to bake bread in a machine—less mess and fuss yet not as much pure fun and joy. After all, making bread from scratch feels so much more satisfying, so much more productive and so much more creative.

To this corporate vice president, baking bread from scratch on a Saturday morning feels so exhilarating and so inspiring. He feels as if his two hands are working hard to bring life to a lifeless wad of flour and water. In fact the vice president says he feels as if he were performing CPR (CardioPulmonary Resusitation) on the chest of the Pillsbury Doughboy. He is kneading him back to life and infusing him with a new found sense of personality if not humanity. A bit far-fetched? Sure, but that's the point.

Waging a personal battle with his own two hands against bread-making machines in particular and technology in general, the vice president demonstrated a key leadership trait: stay grounded. Technology can rob you of your ability to really feel the world around notes Cliff Stoll in his book *Silicon Snake Oil*. He cites the perils of too much technology invading our personal lives. Predictable, you say, until you realize that Stoll is an astrophysicist. His viewpoint is counter-intuitive to our expectations of a Techy and therefore even more poignant and pregnant. When you surrender manual work to a machine, you lose what Stoll calls "the ritual, the sense of accomplishment, the feeling of being a part of the process." Of course he acknowledges that the bread will taste just fine—if a bit too refined—made in a machine instead of baked in an oven. But you miss the best parts of baking bread: "...the feeling of flour between your fingers, kneading the dough, punching the air bubbles, (and) finding a warm place for it to rise. Your friends' grins at the dinner table compliment you, not a machine."

That's why the most effective leaders periodically try to unplug from the grid—at least for a few hours every week. They realize what you lose in efficiency you can gain in effectiveness. They value noodling WITH others at least some of the time rather than Google-ing by themselves most of the time. And the most thoughtful leaders and engaged employees affirm that at times the human touch can be more productive and powerful in the clutch than any machine.

That is the man-over-machine message in the story of chess-playing robot that President Abraham Lincoln often told whenever someone questioned Ulysses S. Grant's ability to lead the army during the Civil War. Lincoln would begin his story by saying that the chess-playing robot had beaten a celebrated player twice.

The celebrated chess expert cried foul at the machine. He wagged his finger and waxed his frustration and anger at the automaton. But then upon closer inspection of the robot he finds something even more disturbing. The losing chess player exclaims in a very derisive tone: "There's a man in it." Exactly. Technology works best when there is a man or a woman in it or behind it. So too in kneading bread or leading others. With a loving touch.

Mint 42

Pre-Serving
Your Golden Eggs

Today's EngageMINT
*Nurture others as a
servant leader.*

braham Lincoln, visiting wounded soldiers during the Civil War, leaned over the hospital bed of one injured soldier and asked: "Is there anything I can do for you? The soldier, not recognizing the president of the United States at his bedside, asked Lincoln to write a letter for him to his mother. The soldier began dictating. And the President began writing. "Mother....I am dying...." Abraham Lincoln knew his role as a Servant Leader: to foster a supportive environment for his troops.

Loving leaders like Lincoln know the value in long-term productive relationships that aren't limited to job descriptions, reporting structures or organizational charts. As Barack Obama noted in concluding his announcement of day he would deliver his last speech to the nation after serving eight years as President of the United States: "For me, it's always been about you." How can you apply that kind of Servant Leadership? Let Larry demonstrate. Larry is more than a mid-level manager in a manufacturing plant. Larry is also a Servant Leader unencumbered by job descriptions or organizational charts especially as employees grow into new roles in new areas of the company.

It's been 11 years since Larry first said good bye and good luck to Doug who was promoted to another part of the company after working directly for Larry for seven years. Yet Larry, the loving leader, still telephones Doug at least once a year on his birthday. "That phone call makes me feel really important," said Doug. As a loving leader, Larry's reputation precedes him wherever he goes. He knows that today, thanks in part to him, there are many productive employees (a.k.a.

geese) throughout the company laying golden eggs of increased productivity and profitability in various departments.So how come there aren't more Larry-The-Loving-Leader types in the work-a-day world nesting and nurturing those golden eggs? Leaders say they are too busy putting out fires. In fact, growing other leaders is listed as the most important objective of all leaders, according to national studies. However, growing other leaders is ranked fourth from the bottom on their to-do list of things that actually get done, according to researchers.

Yet loving leaders make the time to grow other leaders. They understand the overriding dictum that: "Good people are not just crucial to a business, they are the business," notes Richard Branson. And he should know. He is the founder of more billion-dollar companies in more industry segments than any other entrepreneur. People-centric leaders prevail in the marketplace. As former Chrysler chairman Lee Iacocca noted in his biography: "In the end all business operations can be reduced to three words: people, products and profits. People come first. Unless you've got a good team, you can't do much with the other two."

That's why the most effective leaders inherently understand that their teams "are not your people; you are theirs," observes Max De Pree, the former Fortune 500 company CEO in his book *Leadership Jazz.* No wonder loving leaders embrace the insight of author Alexis de Tocqueville in his iconic book *Democracy in America.* He observed that in America business leaders in particular and people in general collaborate. They grow with each other. They sharpen each other like so many knives. And they influence each other's feelings, behaviors and attitudes. He cited the "the reciprocal action of men (and women) where feelings and ideas are renewed, the heart enlarged, and understanding developed." President Abraham Lincoln practiced that kind of "reciprocal action" of, for and by the people. He cared enough to preserve (read pre-serve) the golden eggs to enrich today and enlighten tomorrow, regardless of his job description or reporting relationship on an organization chart.

Mint 43

Stripping Down To Toughen Up

●

Today's EngageMINT
*Break out of your
protective cocoon and fly.*

Y ou just got that big job, that promotion, that major account. And now you are feeling on top of the world. Invincible. You are the King or Queen of the corporate jungle. Hear ME roar! You feel like an elephant: the largest living land animal on earth with no natural predator. So powerful with 50,000 muscles. So awesome. Built like a tank. and just as formidable. No wonder these mighty elephants regularly served as an instrument of war during the reign of the Roman Empire. Yet these 12,000 pound elephants were so vulnerable! How vulnerable? Well consider that the elephant's best friend is the egret — a small bird that rides on the back of an elephant and eats the flies and other insects that "bug" the elephant's sensitive ears. The elephant and the egret, Mother Nature's Odd couple, feed off each other's vulnerabilities and ironically they both become more viable.

Think of that Odd Couple—the egret and the elephant—as a metaphor for the symbiotic relationship between the most loving leaders and their constituents. The most effective leaders do not mask their vulnerabilities. In fact the most effective leaders readily acknowledge their own weakness. They selectively lower their guard to listen more carefully, to learn more comprehensively and ironically to lead more productively. And in becoming more vulnerable, they counter-intuitively get stronger. Leaders realize the more vulnerable they are the more venerable they can become—the more they can be accorded a great deal of respect because of character as the dictionary defines venerable. And the more respect they can command the more real they act, the more trust they can build. And they find the more trust they build, the better they can lead. They realize that a leader's vulnerability can make his or her team even more viable as one leader in a large company noted: "In meetings with my staff, I try to be the first to say that I made a mistake. The more vulnerable I become the more engaged my staff will be." When the leader breaks out of his or her protective cocoon, the entire team flies higher and farther. And often a leader's vulnerability can heighten their personal performance.

Consider Charles Lindbergh—the elephant in any room in aviation circles—embraced his own sense of vulnerability to become the first to fly solo over the Atlantic Ocean and land on the cover of TIME Magazine in 1927 as its first Person of the Year. Seeking greater vulnerability, Lindbergh eschewed putting windows in his plane's cockpit even though windows would have made the plane more aerodynamically sound and more fuel efficient.

But Lindbergh did not want to be insulated—and isolated—from his surroundings. He wanted to be more vulnerable and ultimately more vigilant and more viable. He wanted to feel the wind, smell the sea, and virtually taste the salt in his open cockpit over the ocean to stay even more alert throughout his grueling 33-hour, 3,300-mile flight into the history books from New York to Paris. In figuratively stripping down to toughen up, Lindbergh bared his vulnerability to gain greater performance in much the same way the Sioux Indians would strip down to increase the accuracy of their arrow shooting. The Sioux wore only a loincloth when they hunted buffalo from their horses. With their bare legs they could better grip the horse and more accurately aim and release their arrows on the run.

The lesson is clear: the most effective leaders are ready to strip away their protective cocoons and willing to acknowledge the viability in their vulnerability But first they have to do what all loving leaders do first: acknowledge the elephant in the room: Themselves.

Mint 44

Swallowing Your Feedback
With a Slice of Humble Pie

Today's EngageMINT
*Sweeten your self-awareness
with a slice of Humble Pie.*

You've lost another account. Two staffers are threatening to quit. Your boss has painted a target on your back. And you're forced to listen to some tough love from those around you. You're mad and you're not going to take it anymore. You are so angry! You have only two words for anyone who shovels frustrating feedback in your face as if it were piles of manure. And the last word is YOU. Thank you! "Thank you" is the only appropriate response when people you know and trust offer you a candid assessment of how you are perceived by those around you. That feedback can be hard to swallow, especially from others below you on the organizational chart.

Yet no matter how much you disagree, no matter how defensive you feel, your response as a loving leader is always the same. "Thank you." At least that's the thinking of Alan Mulally, then the CEO of Ford as quoted in Tony Schwartz's book *The Way We're Working isn't Working*. "If someone calls you a son-of-a-bitch take it as a chance to learn," Mulally observed. "Say, thank you very much' for telling me and I'd like to know more about why you think that."

If feedback is the breakfast of champions —a dictum that leadership author Ken Blanchard popularized—then the most effective leaders learn to enjoy their entrée with a side of Humble Pie, even if they don't immediately have the appetite for it. Sure it would be a lot easier to thwart the feedback, to shun the world around you when you're in a world of hurt. But in blocking that feedback you lock yourself into a prison of self-righteous arrogance that turns "innocence into cynicism" and "compassion into callousness" as noted authors Ron Heifetz and Marty Linsky observe in their book *Leadership On The Line*. Executives "who smother dissent ... create an environment of fear and control that turns off the most talented employees and eventually drives them out the door," notes Thomas Neff and James M. Citrin in their book: *You're in Charge, Now What?*" But the most effective leaders see their feedback as specific course corrections they can set to navigate their personal leaderShip for optimum results.

However if your feedback is based only on formal annual reviews, your performance-improving discussion will seem contrived and programmed: checking the box instead of checking in with each other, checking in how you and your boss, or you and your direct reports are building a meaningful and mutually beneficial relationship. That's why the most effective leaders let their guard down. They recognize they are a work in a progress. Leaders realize they must continually reach out beyond their grasp. Forward-looking leaders always have the prospect of continuous self-improvement to continually spark their performance well beyond their expectations. They know they can't get too comfortable.

They know that "healthy relationships require both appreciation and confrontation" as author Susan Scott notes in her book *Fierce Conversations*. They welcome feedback—instructive feedback, constructive feedback, and corrective feedback— without complaint or restraint, knowing that the "highest form of intelligence is to observe without evaluating," (without blaming the messenger or blaming the circumstances), according to Indian philosopher Jiddu Krishnamuranti. Think of giving feedback as a "selfless act" notes author Patrick Lencioni in his book *The Advantage*, "one rooted in a word that I don't use lightly in a business book: love." Indeed, the most effective leaders realize their feedback isn't about them as a person. It's about how others observe their accountability with a caring and sharing mindset. In swallowing your feedback with a slice of Humble Pie, loving leaders reinforce the value others add in evaluating and enhancing overall performance.

Mint 45

POWER LUNCH!
Choking On Your Ego

Today's EngageMINT
*Leaders let others
sit at the head of the table.*

C elebrating a successful product launch, the vice president hosted a lunch for 20 members of his team. Everyone munched on great-tasting sandwiches between celebratory cheers at their favorite deli. After a while, everyone was full of good food and good laughs. Then, the server arrives with a second round of sandwiches for all 21 people in a private dining room. The team members were astonished.

"Who ordered all this?" asked a couple of the team members in unison. "Well, I did," chimed the vice president. "You all deserve it. Job well done." It didn't matter to the vice president that no one at the table wanted another sandwich. Neither did the vice president as it turned out. This afternoon's Power Lunch had little to do with feeding his team members. It had more to do with the vice president feeding his own ego. He ordered another round of sandwiches just because he could. The vice president seemed oblivious to the negative reaction from his team members for the extra sandwich.

So much for his sense of emotional intelligence. And so much for his power-packed inflated view of himself and his expense account that turned a celebration into a confrontation. We all know managers who abuse power and seemingly aren't even aware of it. Their emotional intelligence is so low they see their world only through their narrow point of view and only in their terms. They don't know what they don't know. In seeking an ever-renewing perception of how others perceive them, loving leaders might echo poet Robert Burns lament: "Oh, what some power the Giftee gives us to see ourselves as others see us." But seeing ourselves as others see us is difficult, especially in wielding power in the workplace where sycophants too often find a welcome mat in the leader's office. That's why the most effective leaders learn to walk the line between confidence and arrogance. They know that "it's possible for any leader to get infected with the disease of arrogance and pride and bloat with an exaggerated sense of self," as James Kouzes and Barry Posner observe in their book, *The Leadership Challenge*. Blind spots plague too many leaders as author Jeffrey Pfeffer notes in his book: *POWER, Why Some People Have It and Others Don't*:

> *"It's tough for those*
> *in power to see the world*
> *from others' perspectives,*
> *but if you are going to survive*
> *you need to get over yourself*
> *and your formal position*
> *and retain your sensitivity*
> *to the political dynamics*
> *around you."*

Pfeffer, the professor of organizational behavior at Stanford University's Graduate School of Business, has studied leaders for 30 years. He writes that "it's hard work to keep your ego in check, to constantly be attentive to the actions of others." Especially when you're hungry for more than food. That's why loving leaders always check their egos at the door and let others sit at the head of the table. And that's why the most effective leaders lead with love— described on page 12 (and repeated here for emphasis):

> Leaders lead with a love—a COMPASSION that feeds and feeds off of the feelings of others— feelings that resonate deep inside their souls. They lead with a love—a CONNECTION that stimulates *more listening and learning* for enhanced performance and sparks *more nurturing and encouraging* for increased results. They lead with a love— a CONVICTION that spawns *more humility and vulnerability* and demands more introspection than inspection, knowing that it's all about WE not Me.

Mint 46

JACK NICKLAUS
Tees Up the F-Word: Feelings

●

Today's EngageMINT
Stay true to your character
no matter the distractions.

You may know Jack Nicklaus – the famed Golden Bear– as the greatest professional golfer of all time. But I once got to know a very personal side of Jack Nicklaus light years away from the golf course. And in the process he taught me a lesson in personal leadership and in emotional intelligence that I never forgot: Get in touch with your feelings—especially off the job—so that you can better focus your performance on the job.

It was 1973 and at 33 Jack Nicklaus was at the top of his game. The Golden Bear so dominated the professional golf world that three weeks later he would set the record for winning the most major golf championships— a record that Bobby Jones held for 43 years, a record that Nicklaus still held 43 years later in 2016, a record that includes an incredible 18 victories and an unprecedented 19 second-place finishes in major golf tournaments.

As a newspaper reporter for *The Miami Herald* in Florida, I worked out of the newspaper's West Palm Beach office just 9 miles from Jack Nicklaus' home in North Palm Beach. On Tuesday afternoon, July 24, 1973 The Miami Herald got a news tip from Good Samaritan Medical Center in West Palm Beach that Jack Nicklaus would be visiting the nursery ward to see his fifth born child (Michael) for the first time. My editor assigned me to interview the winner of both the Masters and the US Open just a year before and now the highest paid and most famous golfer in the world. I balked. I told my boss that this was a very personal moment for a dad and his newborn son and that a pesky reporter had no right butting in. But I finally yielded to my boss. Reluctantly, I entered the nursery ward with my photographer. And sure enough there is the Golden Bear — all alone—in front of a glass wall overlooking the newborns. There were no security guards around him. No cameras. No entourage. No hangers on. Jack Nicklaus stood all alone with his thoughts—and feelings—for his newborn son. I stood about 20 feet away hating what I was about to do: invade his privacy. (I needed this job, my first out of college.) Finally, I get enough courage to interrupt Jack's virtual mind meld with his son through the glass wall into the nursery. I introduce myself as a reporter and tell him that I'd like to talk to him about being a dad, about seeing his newborn son for the first time.

Feeling Queasy

His famous blue eyes glazed over me. I could tell he didn't hear a word I said. I backed off. Nicklaus went back to gaga-gooing at the window. Then I approached him again. Once again, I told him who I was and what I was doing there. I was hoping he'd throw me out. (At least then I would have an excuse for my editor.) But Jack surprised me. This time he looked directly into my eyes and said: "Well, what do you want to know?" Then in the corner of the room, I see a nurse standing with a wheelchair ready to go. "I have the smelling salts if you need it, Jack," the nurse bellows. I am thinking this smelling salts comment must be some code for alerting security.

But that didn't happen. Nothing I expected happened on this July afternoon in South Florida. I expected Nicklaus to give me a quasi-pep talk that his newborn son would grow up disciplined, responsible and competitive etc. After all, Nicklaus earned his Golden Bear monicker for his ferocious style of play more than his blond hair—a ferocious style of play that helped him already bag 11 of his 18 major golf tournaments. He had already won four of his 6 masters, three of his 4 US Opens, two of his 5 PGA Championships and two of his 3 (British) Opens. That's why I was surprised to hear Jack Nicklaus—the man with steel nerves who consistently sank 12-foot putts for thousands of dollars— invoke the F-word: Feelings. He said that he felt "queasy in my stomach" when he saw his newborn son for the first time. I was even more surprised to learn that he fainted each time he saw his first four children as newborns. He joked that he spent more time in the recovery room than his wife Barbara did after delivering their third child, Nancy.

At first, I thought Nicklaus was putting me on with all this talk of fainting. I thought he might be having a little fun with a rookie reporter. I made sure he knew I was quoting him. He clearly saw my notebook. Then I asked him why he would want his fans to know that he got sick to his stomach seeing his newborns for the first time. He said: "It's a good human reaction to have." Jack Nicklaus, invoking the F-word — Feelings— clearly saw a teaching opportunity to help other dads get closer to their children, to help other busy executives make more time for their kids.

Nicklaus
Always a Jittery Dad

The headline in the Miami Herald the next day said: ***"Nicklaus Always a Jittery Dad."*** But 20 days later Jack Nicklaus had no jitters on the golf course. He won the PGA Championship and earned THE CREDENTIAL to become professional golf's greatest player. He surpassed Bobby Jones' record for most major championships. Yet, in another salute to his emotional intelligence as a leader in the world of fathers, Nicklaus recalls that same tournament generated his favorite golf photo of all time—ironically without a golf club in his hands.

Jack is photographed carrying his then four-year-old son Gary on his shoulder. Gary came running out onto the 18th green after Jack had just finished the third round. Nicklaus embraced his feelings as a dad even while the nation had a spotlight on him as a sports hero. Nicklaus stayed true to his character, true to himself. His family is his priority even when everyone else is focusing on Jack. Likewise in deciding to grant an interview during such a private moment, Jack Nicklaus focused on inspiring other itinerant dads—road warriors who routinely have to be away from home and, away from their families, on business. He could have brushed off the reporter with a vexing "call my PR people for an interview." He didn't. He could have surrounded himself with an entourage. He didn't. Instead, Jack Nicklaus showed up wearing none of the trappings of his celebrity. And in the process the celebrity-golfer-turned-celebrated dad taught all busy dads a significant personal leadership lesson: ***be true to yourself.*** Be real.

Thirteen years later, Nicklaus was still being true to himself, still unleashing his sharpened emotional intelligence, still focusing on the important not merely the urgent. Then on Sunday April 13, 1986 when his fans were losing their minds as *Sports Illustrated* noted in delirious joy of the improbable, 46-year-old Jack Nicklaus was methodically marching down the back nine recording a six-under par 30 to vault over eight other contenders and become the oldest at the time ever to win the game's most prestigious championship, —The Masters — and teach us all a valuable lesson in leadership:

> *When you are comfortable in your own skin, you can adapt more readily to pressure situations and stay focused amid distractions.*

Nicklaus adapted against the odds. He hadn't won a major tournament in six years or a Masters in 11. And when he came to the 1986 Masters Championship, Nicklaus was already saddled with a plenty of playing baggage: he missed the cut in three of his last seven tournaments. Yet Nicklaus soldiered on, grounded in his strong sense of family and fortified in his own refined sense of emotional intelligence as a loving leader. On and off the golf course.

Wearing Your Mask
To Set The Mood For Leading

●

Today's EngageMINT
*Play the role your audience expects
no matter how uncomfortable.*

Elvis Presley is chatting with Richard Nixon. Mick Jagger is laughing with Donald Trump. And over in the far corner, you could see Madonna dancing with Tom Hanks. Of course this is a masquerade party where real people can step into someone else's shoes for a few hours and dance to a different tune. Ever notice how your body language and mannerisms change whenever you don a mask? That's because you're not simply masking your own identity. You are portraying and projecting another's identity, complete with their gestures. You play the "air guitar" when you don an Elvis Presley mask. You flex your fingers in the air to create "quote marks" when you put on a Richard Nixon mask. In a real sense, the mask you wear gives you permission to act like that character even if it is out of character for you.

That's why in ancient Rome actors wore masks on stage to define their characters and differentiate their personalities. In fact, the word "Persona" means mask in Latin. Each mask featured a kind of megaphone for the actor to speak through to project his personality, to breathe life into his character (even though males also played the female roles).

It's instructive to note that the word— PERSON— comes from the Latin "per" that means "through" and "sonare" that means, "to speak." So a person is literally one who speaks through his or her mask. Of course the most effective leaders realize they wear a mask all the time. It's the face that others see when they look at you for reassurance, for understanding, for a sense of purpose and a clear vision. And too often it's the face that you portray when you are too tired, too frustrated, too angry, and too fearful to look that confident and poised. And yet the leader in you knows that you can't let your troops see or hear your frustration. Not yet. Not now. The most effective leaders know just what kind of mask they need to proverbially don when they need to project poise and sober thought amid chaos. They know just the mask to wear to make others feel more secure, more productive, more creative and more fulfilled. They learn to play a role because they are always on stage. They learn to wear the mask the audience EXPECTS.

Adapting
Without Exploiting

Playing the role the audience expects requires a carefully developed skill in adapting to the needs of the audience without exploiting the situation for one's own benefit. If your employee base–your audience—is frustrated and disheartened in the wake of sluggish sales and a volatile future they need someone to lift their spirits, they need someone to give them hope not hype.

They need someone to don the mask of a caring father figure like President Franklin Delano Roosevelt (FDR) did in speaking sincerely to "my friends" huddled around the radio as if it were a campfire. No wonder the media called his radio addresses fireside chats. Thirty times from 1933 to 1944 through the Great Depression and through World War II FDR spoke so plainly, so personally, so poignantly that historians have written that many Americans felt the President had walked into their living rooms, sat down on the sofa and simply explained the tense issues of the day. The sound of his calm and collected voice seemed like so many compact presses on an open wound. His words, oozing so personally and poignantly through his mask of comfort and confidence, breathed life into a suffocating nation as a loving leader.

SLOOOW DOOOWN!

Throw Your Wait Around

Today's EngageMINT
*Parlay the power
of your patience.*

Attacked as soon as he walked into a dimly lit room, the experienced karate practitioner paused, then stepped back to assess the situation before defending himself. Controlling your instinctive response to defend yourself is easier said than done. Without patience, we can too easily jump to conclusions where our arrogance overshadows our ignorance and where kindness evaporates into rudeness and jealousy.

With patience, leaders become more purposeful. They become like so many Sitting Bulls, the deliberative leader of the Sioux who earned a reputation for his ability to sit and think patiently, listen actively and comprehensively to gain greater understanding and make more targeted and strategic decisions before acting. Yet patience is one of the toughest behaviors to modify in can-do, will-do, result-driven leaders. Even three seconds is too long for nearly 90 percent of leaders to stand still—at least that's the experience in one horse training exercise specifically developed to teach patience to C-suite executives. These executives practice standing still for three seconds so that the leader in them can better grasp the situation and respond more strategically.

How would you do in this test of your patience? You hold the horse with a rope—called aptly a "lead line." You stand about 4 feet in front of the horse. Your task: stand still for a full three seconds so the horse has enough time to learn exactly what you want the horse to do. The horse is trained to react only after three seconds of non-action. Half of the executives start pulling on the lead rope within 2 seconds. Meanwhile most of the other half of the over-eager executives step back to the starting point. Fewer than 1 in 10 learn how to appropriately throw their WAIT around. Lesson learned: Intentions take more than a second or two to be communicated, understood and acted upon. Throw your Wait around. Sloooowwww Dooooowwwn!!!. Become a Sitting Bull. At least for three seconds.

Heed the insight of historian David McCullough, the two-time Pulitzer prize-winning author who prefers to write slowly on a typewriter rather than more efficiently on computer. "I don't want to go faster. I'd really like to go slower if anything," says McCullough. "I like the feeling of throwing that carriage and hearing the bell ring like an old trolley." For those of you who have never even seen a typewriter let alone used one, historians tell us a bell rang when the line you were typing on reached the far right side of the paper. The ring of that bell triggered a Pavlovian response where you instinctively swatted the carriage with your right hand as if you were swatting a fly from right to left.

Other modern-day authors have slowed their writing even more deliberately with a quill pen. James MacGregor Burns used a quill pen to slow down his writing and speed up his thinking process in writing his iconic book in 1978 on transformational leadership titled simply *Leadership.* Burns said he took his cue from the founders of America who all used quill pens. They had to write S-l-o-w-l-y. They had to regularly pause, dip their quill into the ink, and then continue to write. With more patience and purpose and more thought and reflection.

And famed Civil War author Shelby Foote also enjoyed the thrill of the quill. The author of three volumes on the Civil War totaling more than 1.5 million words, Foote would write 500-600 words a day with a dip-pen. "You can only write 3-4 words before you have to dip the pen in the ink again, " Foote said, "I 'm convinced that the most really bad writing in the world is seen under the influence of what's called inspiration." Inspirational writing takes time. So does loving leadership.

Mint 49

TIME-OUT
Gathering Around
The Corporate Campfire
●

Today's EngageMINT
Sharpen your human touch
and recharge your batteries.

Speculation ran rampant. Some thought the company was under siege from a deep-pockets stock holder. Others thought an acquisition was imminent. Still others thought the Chief Executive Officer might be seriously ill. The nine vice presidents were perplexed as they sat in their C-suite conference room awaiting the arrival of the CEO. "Good afternoon and thank you for coming on such short notice," the CEO beamed heartily and healthfully. You could hear half of the room sigh in relief that at least the CEO wasn't ill. Maybe he was resigning?

Finally the CEO set the agenda: "I really appreciate how hard all of you are working. Your efforts are paying off and I want to be sure we take time together to rekindle our fire, to stoke the fire, to maybe even throw another log or two on the fire. So I am calling a regular MANDATORY meeting once every six weeks or so that all us can sit around the camp fire sort of speak for few minutes and take a time out." The vice presidents shrugged their disdain. They haven't got the time to take a time-out like kids in school. The CEO acknowledged their negative sigh, their sense of frustration in being called into a meeting to waste time. But the CEO was adamant in setting his agenda.

First he reminded everyone to turn off their smartphones and tablets. He noted that if there was an emergency during this 45-minute meeting they all would be alerted through his assistant. Then the CEO stood up from his chair and took a firm stance with an even firmer look. He was dead serious: "For the next 20 minutes I am going to ask you to sit in complete silence. Close your eyes if you like and just think. Think of anything at all. It doesn't have to be about work. It's just about you. After 20 minutes, I will ask for volunteers to share anything that's not about work. It could be a new restaurant you discovered. Or something you found in the attic that reminded you of a happy memory. Or something your son or daughter or grandkids said to you that made you smile or that you did together that brightened your day."

Pause for the Cause:
Your Humanity

The executives again shrugged their disdain, shaking their heads in disbelief. But the CEO led by example. He sat down. He took off his watch. He put his hands behind his neck, leaned back in his chair and stared at the ceiling. Others began doodling. All felt awkward. Everyone avoided eye contact. Finally at about the 15- minute mark, the CEO placed his watch on his wrist and said in soft voice:

"Thank you. I know how hard this was to keep still for that long. At least it was tough for me. I hope it gets easier for all of us. But one thing I know there is too much talent in this room to make sure it never burns out, to make sure that we stay fresh." Then the CEO began sharing a story about the first time his dad took him fishing. Another executive recalled the red Corvette he inherited fresh out of college. "What has all this to do with leading effectively?" the CEO questioned.

"Nothing." He paused and then said, "Or everything!" He adjourned the meeting two minutes early. None of the executives were shrugging their disdain any more. A few even seemed to smile.

Were they smirking at the CEO or grinning along with him? It didn't matter. For a few minutes, the CEO slowed the merry-go-around of business to focus more clearly on the linkage between leaders as human beings with personal feelings, hopes and dreams beyond simply as department heads with budgets and staffs to manage and calendars to juggle.

Mint 50

Negotiating a

PEACE of the Action

Today's EngageMINT
Poise under pressure
enhances results.

Acerbic. The name-calling is more vitriolic than ever before. The shouting is getting even louder, the discussion so much more argumentative, and the prospects so much more polarizing. Your negotiating session is on the verge of falling apart. What do you do? Call on a higher power. And get a Peace of the action. That's what Ben Franklin did during the vigorous debate over the philosophy and policy in writing the Constitution of the United States.

The power struggle ensued for five weeks. The largest states wanted representation by population. The smallest states wanted one vote per state to make sure their voices were heard as loudly as the large states. Grid-lock. This Constitutional Congress was on the verge of stalemating at best. Then Ben Franklin gave us all a keen leadership lesson: Cool it when the going gets hot and heavy. Franklin called for a three-day cooling off period. He also proposed that when Congress reconvened the first order of business would be a prayer "to enlighten our minds with a portion of heavenly wisdom, influence our hearts with a love of truth and justice, and crown our labors with complete and abundant success! " The three-day cooling off period worked. The stalemate was resolved. And Congress was formed.

Historians tell us that Franklin was not known as a religious man. But as a leader he understood the power of pausing to take a more deliberative stance that would net a more productive result in negotiations especially when the participants seemed polarized and paralyzed in their own points of view. Sometimes a leader has to take a step back to take a step or two forward. Take a lesson from Phil

Jackson, then the professional basketball coach of the Chicago Bulls playing in the 1994 NBA Eastern Conference National Basketball Association Finals against the New York Knicks. The score is tied with 1.8 seconds remaining in the game. The Bulls call a time out. Jackson devised a play that called for Toni Kukoc to take the final shot. Bulls star player Scottie Pippen, miffed at his coach for not selecting him to take the final shot, refused to play. He sat down on the bench. He deliberately disobeyed an order from the coach to pass the ball to Kukoc. The Bulls had to execute the final play (and win) without Pippen.

Cool It
to Better Do It

The Chicago Bulls won much more than a game that night. They won a greater sense of commitment to each other thanks to Jackson's poised leadership especially in the locker room following the game. Jackson was fuming mad at Pippen. (How would you feel if your star employee deliberately disobeyed a direct order at a crucial time?) The entire team gathered in the locker room after the game. They expected Jackson to unleash his frustration with a verbal dressing down and a gargantuan bite out of Pippen's wallet for his blatant insubordination. Instead, Jackson took a page out of Ben Franklin's "Cool-It" playbook: Jackson calmly looked at the faces of each player and said: "What happened has hurt us. Now you (the entire team) have to work this out." Then Jackson walked out of the locker room. He methodically smothered his own ego in favor of the team's more collaborative and ultimately more productive result: restoring trust in each other and pledging individual responsibility to each other.

Ben Franklin would have been proud. Phil Jackson called on a higher power and got a <u>Peace</u> of the action.

Leaders WOW 'em
With a Feeling

Today's EngageMINT
Instill the thrill more than
instruct the drill.

Beaming proudly, the dad thrusts a new fishing rod into the tiny hands of his seven-year-old son. "Here's how you fish," he instructs. The boy dutifully follows his dad's commands. And sure enough, the boy eventually would catch a fish— but not the thrill of fishing. And soon the boy abandoned his fishing pole for a swimming hole. Meanwhile his seven-year-old cousin wielding a fishing pole for the first time was having fun even if he wasn't catching any fish. He was too busy enjoying the WOW in fishing to concentrate on the how of fishing. The WOW? His dad's WOW words still echoed in his mind: "Think of your fishing pole as a magic wand that you dip into a watery wonderland." This boy was dangling a magic wand around some fish. Not fishing. And that made all the difference in maintaining his attention and focusing his performance.

That's what loving leaders do. They instill the WOW while others demonstrate only the HOW in performing a task. WOWing leaders weave more meaning and purpose in helping others get comfortable with new things, new technologies, and new methods for getting things done. WOWing leaders weave together the threads of personal confidence and conviction to help others grasp and embrace change.

Without weaving the WOW, you can instruct but not instill. Without weaving the WOW, you can grip its utility but not grasp its potential. Without weaving the WOW, you can understand its basic features but not realize its latent value. But a loving leader weaving the WOW can influence others to follow their inherent passion and achieve their creative best rather than blindly comply to someone's instructions and settle for less. How do you WOW others? You don't lean in. You step back and view the experience from the other's point of view. You don't try to push your message. You help others pull on your message and bring it to themselves. That counter-intuitive behavior takes character based on an "inverse logic," according to author David Brooks in his book *The Road to Character.* To gain that creative dimension—that WOW factor—leaders must first learn how to forget themselves, how to lose themselves, how to surrender themselves and how to give themselves to others according to these four tenets of "inverse logic" that Brooks defines:

1. *FORGET yourself in order to fulfill yourself.*
2. *LOSE yourself to find yourself.*
3. *SURRENDER something outside of yourself to gain strength within.*
4. *GIVE in order to receive.*

Anchored in that character of "inverse logic," leaders realize the bottom-line in leadership "isn't how far we advance ourselves but how far we advance others," observes John Maxwell in his book, *21 Irrefutable Laws of Leadership.* In his Law of Connection, Maxwell adds: "Effective leaders know that you have to touch people's hearts before you ask them for a hand." To touch their people's hearts, leaders WOW 'em. They create a more compelling context for their content. Together they develop the WOW long before the how.

In WOW-ing others, the most effective leaders sell more than tell. They become like the doctor lecturing medical school students on using a stethoscope, citing the art as much as the science. He put his ordinary lecture content into a more visually stimulating and a more memorable context. He noted that listening to a heart murmur is like listening to "the wind rustling through golden corn in a kind of poetry." Like the lecturing doctor, loving leaders brandish their magic wands with a flair for igniting the imagination that one can feel as much as see. And WOW 'em!

Mint 52

SCREENED OUT
Beware of Hiding Behind Your Technology

Today's EngageMINT
Be effective not just efficient in using technology.

Crowds seemingly thundered into the large retail store while busy cashiers conducted a scanning symphony of sound and fury. One cashier seemed more tired than usual. And no wonder. She was so busy she worked through her break. So focused on the robotic routine of scanning and bagging, she hardly noticed that no other cashier came to relieve her after two hours as customary. But now after nearly three hours of standing, scanning and cashiering, her aching knees and blurry vision demanded she stop and take a rest regardless that her check-out lane was still streaming with shoppers. Finally, she hit the emergency button on her cash register to summon her supervisor.

However, her supervisor was just as busy, too busy to realize that she was an hour late in relieving her cashier for her much needed 15-minute break. The embarrassed supervisor finally wormed her way through customers to reach the cashier who looked at her supervisor with pleading eyes. But instinctively her supervisor looked down into her hand-held device to validate the cashier's claim of a late break. She couldn't believe that her technology failed her. She thought there is no way her technology in the palm of her hand would have allowed the supervisor to make this kind of mistake: failing by nearly 60 minutes to send this valued veteran employee on her well-deserved break.

Inadvertently, the supervisor added insult to injury and the cashier vented her frustration: "Wait a minute. Wait a minute," demanded the cashier. "I just told you that I have been here for nearly three hours and the first thing you do is check your (hand-held) computer. No way. I deserve more respect than that." Finally, the supervisor realized her mistake and immediately brought in another cashier. It would be a few more hours before that supervisor would apologize to the cashier for missing her break.

That supervisor learned a lesson that the most effective leaders learn: beware of relying too much on the efficiency of your technology. Beware of letting your screens screen you out of developing meaningful relationships that can become both productive and profitable. Give your employees more face time. Efficiency is good. Effectiveness is even better especially when initiatives in the spirit of efficiency distort the bottom line and undermine humanity.

Manning
the Man-ual

Consider the fictional chief executive officer who purchased a machine that could virtually run every job in his factory. Thousands of jobs were eliminated in a salute to efficiency where "two machines can replace 114 workers." Finally, when the chief engineer loses his job to the machine, he confronts the CEO: "I'm a man—and that makes me better than that hunk of metal. Bettttterrrr!!!!!"

That *Twilight Zone* episode on television in the 1960s still hits a nerve of every entrepreneur trying to balance people issues and bottom-line realities. Fittingly, even the chief executive officer in that foreboding episode of The *Twilight Zone* is replaced by a machine. Yet the most effective leaders—loving leaders—know that no machines, no robotics, no technology can operate without a MANual.

Mint 53

Creating a Comfort Zone:
FOR OTHERS

Today's EngageMINT

*Lay down a welcome mat
for your office visitors.*

Mightily, the Siberian Tiger stares powerfully yet mysteriously on the wall directly in front of the CEO's desk. The limited edition print from Andy Warhol's *Endangered Species* collection stands guard over the CEO—a constant reminder to the CEO to stay vigilant in order to survive in the jungle of today's highly-competitive business terrain.

Yet a placid waterfall watercolor painting flows lazily from the wall immediately behind the CEO. It's a soothing scene that sprays a proverbial comforting mist to cool down even the most hot-tempered or stressed-out visitors seated directly across from the CEO. All by design. The most effective leaders exhibit an art for creating a more conducive environment to do business. And that often includes the collection and display of significant works of art in the CEO's office. Let's call it a Comfort Zone for others where visitors can articulate their issues more calmly and more clearly. Picture the environment in this CEO's office: Refreshing yet reinforcing. Soothing yet stringent. Peaceful yet powerful. Entering the office, the CEO sees and feels the soothing water fall. But then sitting behind her desk, the CEO looks up and is reminded of poet William Blake's observation of The Tiger:

*Tiger, tiger, burning bright
In the forests of the night. What immortal*

*hand or eye
could frame thy fearful symmetry?*

The leadership lesson is clear: The Tiger is focused on gaining turf, on ruling the jungle just as the CEO must be focused on guarding and guiding the fortunes of the company through a vast array of competitive pressures. And that takes art—the art of leadership. That art of leadership of course is inherent in the leader's own ability to cool down tense situations in his or her office, especially in often contentious open-door policy meetings when disgruntled employees seek retribution from a higher authority. Here's how one humble and poised leader —a.k.a. a loving leader— summarily disarmed his nervous or angry plaintiffs with a sense of humor. A woman factory worker with a checkered 12-year history with the company had complained her way to the top of the company for the first time. The CEO was briefed. He was ready. He invited her to take a seat at his marble table. He sat down, smiled and then got up to shut his office door. He sat back down and pointed to the door and said in a soft comforting voice: "That's just in case you start yelling at me we won't bother anyone." He smiled. She smiled. The CEO put the factory worker at ease.

They discussed her concerns over her working environment in general and her strained working relationship with her supervisor. The CEO listened. He empathized with her point of view. And then in soft comforting voice the CEO ruled as he had done in 90 percent of the open-door meetings he held over the years: against the employee. He explained his decision. She walked out of his office with mixed feelings. She wished she had persuaded the CEO that she was right all along. But at least she felt valued. She felt as if someone in top management was willing to "hear my side of it." She personally had experienced the Comfort Zone in the CEO's office. Five years later that employee was still working for the company and every Christmas since then the CEO got a big box of freshly baked homemade Italian cookies from that same employee. Call it Comfort food for a loving leader's Comfort Zone.

Mint 54

REWARDING:
Way Beyond Awarding

Today's EngageMINT
*Beware of turning a slap on the back
into a kick in the ass.*

Summond into the top editor's office for the first time in years, the reporter's blood pressure rose and his heart began beating a bit faster. He thought it could only be bad news. He must have screwed up. Or worse: he was getting fired. Instead the editor reached into his desk before the reporter could sit down. The editor quickly tossed a small plastic bag toward the reporter who instinctively put up his right hand and snared it right out of the air. For a second, he thought it might be a bag of pot that someone planted in his desk.

But then he gripped the bag and to his sheer relief it was anything but soft and powdery. No this was hard and gleaming with a golden flair. Then suddenly the booming voice of the editor cut through the tension. "Here, I am supposed to give you that," harrumphed the editor. The reporter opened his right hand and found himself holding a 5-year-service pin for his five years of experience working for that newspaper. The reporter sighed in relief as the editor took a phone call and dismissed the reporter with a wave of his hand.

The young reporter left the editor's office feeling more like castigating someone than celebrating with anyone. A slap on the back had turned into a kick in the proverbial ass. And yet from the editor's point of view, he accomplished his goal. He awarded the 5-year pin as if it was his to give based on the calendar instead of rewarding the employee for something he rightfully earned based on his disciplined performance over that same calendar's five years. But it didn't have go down like this. That gold five-year pin presentation could have left a pleasing taste in both the editor and the reporter if only the editor knew what loving leaders know: the difference between rewarding and awarding. In rewarding, loving leaders define, differentiate and distinguish a particular employee's specific contribution more personally, more privately, and more sincerely. In rewarding more than simply awarding, loving leaders realize the distinction between awards and rewards:

Awards are presented.
Rewards are earned.
Awards are event oriented.
Rewards are individually centered.
Awards honor past performance.
Rewards incent future performance.

Event-oriented awards bring together diverse audiences who have a single interest such as the Oscars. Award shows are platforms for the presenters as much as showcases for the performers. Award shows always reflect upon the awarder as much as the awardee. Rewards require only an audience of one. And a loving leader who cares. Personally. Sincerely. And most of all, individually.

In rewarding purposefully rather than simply awarding popularly, loving leaders stay focused on the individual stars that comprise the constellation. They never allow the general population in a given group to obscure the individual people in the group. As US Army General Norman Schwarzkopf observed: "I have seen competent leaders who stood in front of a platoon and all they saw was a platoon. But great leaders stand in front of a platoon and see it as 44 individuals, each of whom has aspirations, each of whom wants to live, each of whom wants to do good."

And each of whom who wants to be rewarded personally by a loving leader: a loving leader who treats others with dignity and respect, a loving leader who recognizes and appreciates the specific contribution of others, and a loving leader who rewards personally more than simply awards perfunctorily.

Mint 55

ACCOUNTABILITY
Making a 200% Trust Investment

●

Today's EngageMINT
*Fully share responsibility and accountability
with your business partners.*

Quick quiz. For an effective partnership, how much of an investment beyond financial terms should each partner make: 50-50 percent sounds about right, doesn't it? Not to a leader like General Norman Schwarzkopf, who led the United States and its allies to victory in the Desert Storm in 1991. Forget the quid pro quo 50-50 (percent) focus that by definition places limits on each partner's investment in time and attention to the business at hand. Instead think 100-100 percent total commitment from both partners advises Schwarzkopf. That comprehensive sense of accountability (a total of 200 percent) is the mindset of loving leaders.

Loving leaders think of their business partnership as if it were a marriage. Your business marriage demands total and complete attention to each other. And when that business spawns a new product or service your business marriage demands a 10-fold increase in attention from both partners. At least that's the way Schwarzkopf saw it. "Marriage is not 50-50 (percent). That's baloney. It's 100-100 percent. And in raising kids it's 1000-1000 (percent)!" That's because both partners (a.k.a. loving leaders) take FULL responsibility for their marriage. They BOTH are responsible and accountable not only for their own personal behaviors but also for the behaviors of their respective partners and for the behaviors of their children. No partner can delegate their responsibility to the other even on the basis of a lack of expertise, knowledge or experience in a given area. They are still both accountable. Love "begins with one absolute condition: unlimited liability," observes Robert K. Greenleaf in his book, *Servant Leadership.* "As soon as one's liability for another is qualified to any degree, love is diminished by that much." And the author of *5 Dysfunctions of a Team* Patrick Lencioni says: "If we love someone—and I hope all of you love the people who work for you—you owe it to them to hold them accountable even if they don't love you back for it." No wonder Viktor Frankl, the author and professor of psychiatry, advocated supplementing the Statue of Liberty on the east coast with a Statue of Responsibility on the west coast. "Freedom is in danger of degenerating into mere arbitrariness unless it lives in terms of responsibleness," Frankl observed.

Claiming Responsibility

With a sense of collective responsibility, loving leaders heed the call of Nobel Prize winner Alexander Solzhenitsyn where, "the salvation of mankind lies only in making everything the concern of all." That making everything the concern of all—that embedded sense of commitment—is the crux of every successful initiative for BOTH partners. Neither waits for the other to take the lead. They both assume the lead and then work out their plan together on who does what, when. That's why credibility is critical in building a viable and mutually satisfying relationship that is more open to persuasion and greater understanding of the other's point of view. As the legendary broadcast news anchor Edward R. Murrow once observed:

> *"To be persuasive, we must be believable.*
> *To be believable, we must be credible.*
> *To be credible, we must be truthful."*

And to be truthful each partner gives their all in parlaying a collective 200% commitment to each other with love— defined by philosopher Milton Mayeroff as "the selfless promotion of the growth of others." Response-ably. And account-ably.

Mint 56

ATTRACTION
Turning Harm Into Charm

Today's EngageMINT
*Strengthen viability
with creative connections.*

Oweee, Oweee," the four-year-old screamed after diving into a swimming pool just chemically-cleaned. "My eyes burn." The little girl found out just how toxic chlorine can be even in small doses. Chemists tell us that in high concentrations, chlorine can be dangerous. In fact, by itself chlorine can be caustic. But if you combine chlorine with something else, for example sodium, the resulting compound is something that's very tasty on popcorn and hundreds of others foods: table salt. Different connection. Different association. Different affinity.

Making new and even more vital connections. That's what leaders do. They make innovative connections that turn potentially dangerous elements into creatively productive solutions. They turn potential harm into a potent charm. They take something generic and add a new connection, a new element, and make what was once bland at best or dangerous at worse even more grand, even more valuable and even more viable. Consider sterling silver. It is not pure silver. Pure silver would be too soft for use as table ware. So sterling silver is mixed with copper making sterling silver more viable and valued. Consider 24-karat gold. It is not pure gold. Pure gold would be too soft for use in creating rings. So 24-karat gold is mixed with copper making 24-karat gold more viable and valued.

In their drive to make those durable and value-added connections, leaders feed—and feed off of—others. Loving leaders know the power in physically connecting with others, in interacting with others, and in being present as much as possible amid a world of Skype and hype. Loving leaders know the closer they associate with their teams the better they both perform. They become like the strings on a guitar played on a single cradle rather than each string played on a different cradle. Played together with such proximity to each other their strings reverberate off each other with a more robust sound. And together they resonate in unison with more verve and reverb than a single string.

Leaders realize that the proximity to what or to whom you surround yourself with affects you much like pendulum clocks that will synchronize without any manual or electronic intervention when placed collectively in the same room. Likewise proximity to your neighbors matters in much the same way that the South Pole is colder than the North Pole.

Scientists tell us that the South Pole is colder largely because of the geography of its nearest neighbors: the cold oceans that surround the South Pole. However the North Pole's nearest neighbors—land masses—are a bit more neighborly, a bit warmer since land retains heat longer than water. So the North Pole is warmer than the South Pole primarily because of the associations it has made albeit without much choice.

But leaders have plenty of choices to make new connections, new associations. They can break away from a cold climate into a warmer working environment. That's why most effective leaders are always evaluating the need to make different and potentially more viable connections in steering their personal careers and in stirring new ideas, products and services in their organizations.

The leadership lesson is clear: leaders leading with love are the salt of the earth. They make the right connections at the right time much in the same way that copper strengthens gold or silver for greater viability.

PART III

CONVICTION

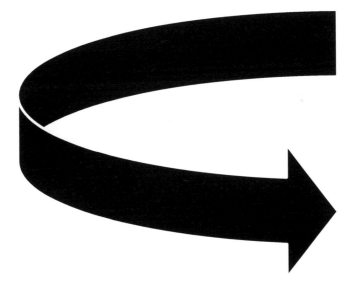

"Why can't work be fun?
What if we could inspire people
in such a way
so that each day
they would be
enthusiastic
about their roles and motivated
to use their gifts, and
what if
we could have the
insight and ability
to recognize those gifts and
to show our appreciation in
return?"

--Bob Chapman, CEO, Barry-Wehmiller
and author of *Everybody Matters*

Mint 57

Wearing Your **BVDs** *in Public*

Today's EngageMINT
*Stand for something
or fall for anything.*

Smashing his Stradivarius-sounding violin on stage, the accomplished musician stunned his audience. Then he calmly explained that he had been playing a cheap violin he had purchased at a pawnshop. "I smashed that violin to prove to you that performance is based inside the person not inside the instrument," he said.

So is leadership. Your leadership is already in you. Your task is to express it, to play the music already vibrating in your soul so that it resonates with your followers. And together you dance to same music and collectively with your followers you keep the organization in tune and in rhythm with the times. No one or nothing else can define your brand of leadership. You can't brandish it with a uniform or logo. You can't cloak yourself in prestige and power. You can only stand in public wearing only your BVDs, for all to see. Your BVDs are who you are underneath it all:

B for **Beliefs**.
V for **Values**.
D or **Disciplines**.

Beliefs are critical in cementing your convictions. As Max De Pree writes in his book: *Leadership is an Art*: "Managers who have no beliefs but only understand methodology and quantification are modern day eunuchs." Ouch! The dictionary says that a eunuch is a man who has had his sexual organs removed. Secondary definitions underscore the political futility of a eunuch as one who lacks virility or power. Even though De Pree's observation four decades ago is obviously sexist and hardly politically correct, the concept is still valid. Leaders without beliefs call into question their personhood, their humanity, their manhood or womanhood. Indeed, if a leader can't stand up for something they believe in public wearing only their BVDs— in the parlance of the iconic underwear brand—then no follower can stand with them. Without people standing with you or following you, you can't lead.

That's why the most effective leaders first discern their beliefs, their values and their disciplines before embarking on becoming a leader. Then they solemnly and soberly take what Jeff Immelt, the CEO at General Electric, calls a "journey into their soul." They first explore what interests them, what sparks their passion, what drives their thinking, what heightens their vision, what invigorates their involvement and what ultimately validates their existence.

With those beliefs well–rooted the most effective leaders are more apt to define the line in the sand where they will make their stand and attract others to their bandstand. With those beliefs well anchored in their conviction they erect bumper guards on their own bowling lanes of the mind to make sure they always stay out of the gutters and on the road to success. After all, it is "impossible to expect people to extend the Golden Rule very far if they are unmoored, unanchored and insecure themselves," as Thomas Friedman writes in *Thank You for Being Late.*

Standing in their BVDs, the most effective leaders are bathed in greater confidence, awash in even more courage and showered in a growing commitment. They embrace the passionate and inspiring notion of author and French poet Antoine de Saint Exupery who observed: "If you want to build a ship don't drum up the men to gather wood, divide the work and give orders. Instead teach them to yearn for the vast and endless sea." With those beliefs well-conceived and with those convictions well-anchored, leaders heighten their vision, invigorate their involvement and ultimately validate their capability. Loving leaders in particular know ONLY they can enunciate their beliefs, their values and their disciplines. And only you as a loving leader can illustrate who you are underneath it all. With conviction!

Mint 58

Turning the Habitual Into a Ritual

Today's EngageMINT
*Focus on helping others
to help yourself.*

Only one tired and very frustrated office worker remained in the office building at 11:30 pm. He was bored with his routine and tedious long day at work. He heard the janitor cheerfully humming and whistling while he dumped waste paper baskets in an adjacent conference room. The janitor wasn't listening to any music. No iPod. No Mp3 player. His happy tune, beaming straight from his heart and soul to his bright and beaming voice, irked the lone office worker even more until he couldn't stand it anymore. He unleashed his frustration on the janitor: "Frank, how can you be so happy doing a routine job like that? The janitor looked deep into the tired eyes of the office worker and responded:

*"I have too important
a job to get frustrated by it."*

The office worker's face flared. The happy, humming janitor, politely added:

*"I do have an important
job. It's so important that if I don't
do my job tonight, you can't do your
job tomorrow."*

Frank—the-janitor—had discovered a purpose to his work, a purpose that generated fortitude in the face of frustration, a purpose that turned the ho-hum into the gung-ho, a purpose that turned the blah into a-Ah HA!. Frank —the janitor—was right of course. No office worker could work in an environment where dust blankets the furniture, where dirt and grime chew up the floors, and where waste paper baskets brim with banana peels, milk cartons and half-eaten sandwiches. Frank—the-janitor—turned the routine into the pristine; the habitual into a ritual and the mechanical into the magical. Martin Luther King Jr., must have had someone like Frank—the janitor—in mind when he spoke of the dignity in all work and the pride in all workers. "If a man is called to be a street sweeper, he should sweep streets even as Michelangelo painted or Beethoven composed music or Shakespeare wrote poetry," Rev. King said. Frank—the janitor—did his job on purpose with the precision of a Michelangelo and with the passion of a Beethoven. Exaggerated? Way over the top? Sure, but that's the point. Frank—the janitor—personified what poet Kahlil Gibran felt when he observed:

> *"When you work, you are like a flute*
> *through whose heart the whispering of*
> *the hours turns to music."*

Frank—the-janitor—was that flute. He played his broom as if it were a flute. On key. On target. And on purpose for others. Frank, the janitor, understood and embraced the Harvard business school insight that all business is an "exercise in empathy" since the purpose of business is to solve a problem, according to Harvard's Clay Christensen more than simply to create a customer as management guru Peter Drucker cited or to maximize profits as economist Milton Friedman observed. Celebrating business as an exercise in empathy is evident in artist John Singleton's Copley 1768 painting of Paul Revere as a silversmith. Seven years before taking his famous ride into the history books, Revere is seen taking pride in a teapot he just crafted. His labor of love for others reflects the empathetic thoughts of author Henry David Thoreau who said that success usually comes to those too busy to be looking for it. After all, they're too busy helping others. On purpose.

In fact, loving leaders are busy helping others so they don't slip on the proverbial banana peels; too busy turning the habitual into a ritual and too busy whistling while they work to throw another log on the Fire of Frustration no matter how tired they are or how routine their work. After all, they're on a mission. For others.

Mint 59

Earning Your
METTLE of HONOR

●

Today's EngageMINT
Action is the traction
to climb Mount Happiness.

Surely, the professor would cancel the class. Why should he commute 100 miles round trip —twice a week—on snowy country roads in the dead of winter for only two students? The professor knew why. And 10 years later so did the rest of the world. That's when both of his students in that class at the University of Chicago—Chen Ning Yang and Tsung-Dao Lee— won the Nobel Prize in physics. Loving leaders like Professor Subrahmanyan Chandrasekhar, Ph.D., follow their convictions without regard to economies of scale or personal convenience. They charge down the road of achievement with a kettle full of mettle— a kettle full of "vigor and strength of spirit" as the dictionary defines "mettle."

And it pays off.

Thirty-six years later, Professor Chandrasekhar also won the Nobel Prize in Physics in 1983. That spirit of conviction, that spirit of self-less service, that spirit of total dedication marks the most effective leaders. They walk the talk in real time and share their spirit, energy and drive— their love. Without reservation.

Consider Mohandas Gandhi. He never held any official leadership position. He had no wealth. He commanded no armies. Yet he earned his mettle of honor and mobilized millions, according to author Keshavan Nair in his book *A Higher Standard of Leadership*. Nair noted the magnetic appeal of Gandhi's mettle: "People were willing to serve with him—and for him— because his life was devoted to serving them." He was devoted to helping them find meaning in their lives, as author Harold Kushner notes in reinforcing the contribution of the most effective leaders:

"Our souls are not hungry for fame, comfort, wealth or power. Those create almost as many problems as they solve.

"Our souls are hungry for meaning, for the sense that we have figured out how to live so that our lives matter, so that the world will be at least a bit different for our having passed through it."

That's what the love of a leader is all about: helping others grow as author and psychiatrist Viktor Frankl says in his book *Man's Search for Meaning.* Leaders are always on the move—forward-looking and continuously improving. They are never satisfied. They are always striving and never arriving. Each finish line is a starting line. Consider the CEO who turned Kimberly-Clark around and beat the competition in six of eight categories. In retirement Darwin Smith reflected on his personal performance as quoted in Jim Collins' book *Good to Great:* "I never stopped trying to become qualified for the job."

No wonder that most pioneers who raced across the country in the 1849 Gold Rush said that even if they found all the riches they would ever need, they would continue to pan for gold. It is the PURSUIT of happiness not the happiness itself that sparked our forefathers' spirit of independence as those loving leaders of yesteryear clarified in the Declaration of Independence: "in the pursuit of life, liberty and happiness."

Action is the traction to climb Mount Happiness. Maybe that's why a chairman of a large corporation has a sign on his desk that reads: "A desk is a dangerous place from which to watch the world." Loving leaders take action. Even on snowy country roads. Driving and striving with conviction!

Mint 60

ON DUTY 24/7
Professing Your Professionalism

Today's EngageMINT
Leaders serve others
always in all ways.

Heading back to the airport from another exhausting business trip, you see an "Off-Duty" light beaming atop another taxi cab. You fantasize: "Oh if only I could install one of those off-duty lights in my office or workstation." Absurd? Of course. Leaders are always on duty, 24/7. As PROFESSionals, leaders consistently profess their personal conviction that they are doing what they were meant to do, 24/7. There is music within their hearts and souls to play wherever they are no matter what day or time of day.

That's why historians tell us that: Archimedes made his mathematical music in the bathtub. O. Henry made his literary music while in a bar in New York City, writing *Gift the Magi*. Adam Smith made his economic music at the British Coffee House in London, writing *The Wealth of Nations*. Thomas Edison made his electronic music in the baggage car on a railroad train, conducting experiments. And Jack Norworth made his music on a train in 1908, writing Take *Me Out to the Ball Game*—still the most popular song sung at baseball parks.

In making music on the job 24/7, professionals showcase their emotional decree TO the job beyond their educational degree for the job. They approach their profession as a leader with the mind-set of a physician or an attorney as a practice, a discipline with core prerequisites applied differently according to patient or client need. And like a practice in medicine or law, a leader's job is always in process, always seeking continued improvement in all ways and often seeking continuous improvement with an on-going, never-ending religious fervor that turns the ordinary into the extraordinary. George Washington Carver concentrated his religious fervor on the peanut. He invented more than 300 different uses for the peanut, saying that his success stemmed from his "love of the peanut." Ray Kroc, in founding the McDonald's hamburger empire, focused his passion on the French fry. He noted that "the French Fry has become almost sacrosanct for me. Its preparation is a ritual to be followed religiously."

In making music on the job 24/7 these loving leaders with a professional zeal and a steady keel demonstrate a work spirit "that everything they have ever done contributes to what they are doing now," notes Sharon Louise Connelly, author of *Work Spirit, Recapturing the Vitality of Work*. They have "a feeling of doing something of value and making contributions, a sense of connections with people in the universe and a feeling of doing work they are meant to." Even in the face of hard times.

Consider the professionalism of Walt Disney during a hard time when he was 21. He was down but not out. He had to file for bankruptcy. So what that his business had just failed? He didn't fail. His wings were trimmed not clipped. He felt like the bird that Victor Hugo described, "pausing in its flight on boughs too light, feels them give away yet sings knowing she hath wings." Confidently he acted on his convictions and purchased a one way first-class train ticket to Los Angeles in search of his next job.

Loving leaders, professing their professionalism, have wings of fortitude in the face of frustration. They know their "self-worth cannot be verified by others" as Dr. Wayne Dyer wrote in *Your Erroneous Zones*. "You are worthy because you say it is so." You are worthy because you profess worthiness as a professional, 24-7. And you earn credibility for your capability from those you serve professionally as a loving leader, 24-7. Wherever you are. With conviction!

Mint 61

Leading With Your
Best Foot Forward

Today's EngageMINT
*No one is
too big to fail.*

Awesome. The floor-to-ceiling picture of a 257-foot Sequoia tree planted in the CEO's office seemed to scream to all visitors:

> *"BEHOLD-All -Ye-Who-Enter.*
> *This is Command Central of the Largest,*
> *The Biggest, and The Tallest Company*
> *in the World in our Industry."*

However, this CEO had another idea in mind when he showcased the massive life-like photograph of the tallest tree in the world on a 12-foot tall wall in his office. That photograph became a meaningful and memorable teaching tool to reinforce the company's mission as the BEST in the industry not merely the biggest. The CEO argued his best vs. biggest case most significantly —and visually— whenever he met with a candidate for a leadership position in the company. Invariably, the candidate would see that soaring Sequoia in the photograph and say something about the thrill of working for the biggest company in the industry. And that triggered the CEO's teaching moment.

Instinctively, the CEO climbed up on his proverbial soapbox: "Our focus is on being the best not the biggest," the CEO would intone and then point to the huge framed photograph— 9 feet tall and 3 feet wide—dominating his office. Then he'd stand up and invite his captive audience of one to view the photo up close before launching into his well-rehearsed, often repeated, statistical barrage on the largest living things on earth. "Take a look at that Sequoia tree. It is as tall as a 25-story building or more," the CEO began as if introducing a documentary film on the awe and majesty of Mother Nature's tallest wonder of the world. "The Sequoia tree is so big it weighs as much as 14 blue whales—the largest known animal to have ever existed. In fact, a Sequoia tree would need a belt 100 feet long to cover its girth and three parking places to plant its footprint." The CEO was on roll now. He noted some Sequoia trees are still growing (around if not up) 3,000 years later at Sequoia National Park in Nevada and California. Gravity keeps these trees from growing much taller than 300 feet, but virtually nothing stops the tree from growing its girth, "a lot like humans" the CEO said, tugging at his belt. He paused for effect.

Then he walked back to his desk, sat down and sharpened his teaching point as his captive audience of one settled back into his chair: BIG does not infer best. Big could also mean brittle. He said that after more than 30 centuries the wood of a Sequoia tree is so brittle it shatters when it crashes to the ground and can only be used to build match sticks or shingles.

Beware of Becoming
Too Insulated

Being the biggest can become a burden, the CEO explained. No one is too big to fail. He said when you're big, you can become too insulated, too protected. He noted the three feet of bark on a Sequoia tree is so thick, it's virtually fire-proof, rot-proof, and bug proof. The CEO noted that with all that insulation —and isolation from the "real" world— your head is likely to grow even more than the tree and then your arrogance will more likely blind your judgement.

Then as an emerging leader you could become foolishly embolden like the 9-foot giant of biblical fame. Goliath was so big, he merely laughed at a young boy armed only with a stone and a sling shot. But David knew better. Like all loving leaders, he knew he only had to lead with his BEST foot forward. Not his biggest as long as he performed up to his expectations. With conviction!

Mint 62

Pulling Your Own Strings

Today's EngageMINT
*Stay connected to your values
no matter how far you wander.*

Yo-yos—flanking the side of the Chief Executive Officer's desk like so many-colored safety switch buttons— quickly became a conversation piece for every first time visitor. And whenever he saw that familiar quizzical look, the CEO was only too happy to share the yo-yo lore that turned his desk into a toy chest of sorts. To this CEO, yo-yos are too important to be used only as toys or as negative reminders of simplistic observations on cyclical variance that every dieter knows only too well: what goes down eventually comes up and what goes out eventually comes back. The visitor learns that the yo-yo display on his desk was a gift from his direct reports when he first joined the company as CEO. They were intrigued with his concept of principle-centered, values-based leadership that he referenced in his first speech to the company.

"The most effective leaders are like yo-yos," the CEO declared to surprised looks in his company-wide audience assessing their new leader for the first time. *"Leaders by definition,"* the CEO explained, *"are always attached to something. They always come with strings attached. Strings of cultural norms and behaviors. Strings of values and truths. Strings that make you, you."*

Yet these leaders are not bound by these strings, he continued. They are tethered to a life support system of sorts that counter-intuitively sets them free. Free to explore new frontiers. Free to wander out beyond their comfort zones. Free to create Loop the Loop and Around the World and other innovations. And free to return to their ground zero whenever they want, the CEO further explained. But no matter how far they roam, the most effective leaders stay attached to their value system. In fact the CEO said it is their value system — their attached strings—that makes it possible for leaders to expand their comfort zone into more creative and more productive arenas that heighten performance.

Stay Attached No Matter How Far You Roam

They pull their own strings by design with a focused sense of purpose and professional pride. They embrace the notion of having a fixed point in their lives. They know that "putting one's shoulder to the wheel presupposes a patch of solid ground to stand on," as author Allen Wheelis observes in his book *The Quest for Identity.* But that solid ground must be constantly worked the CEO added: "It's not enough to have a shiny yo-yo with a snappy string attached, if you don't continuously work at it, continuously improve it and continuously innovate it. From a fixed point. Leaders know that the yo-yo is a tool more than a toy, a tool that requires a hands on, fully engaged experience. And that tool requires added accountability and responsibility to keep learning from your failures and from your successes with a strong attention to detail. The CEO added:

> *"When you fail in performing a yo-yo trick, you have to physically wind that string back into the heart and soul of the yo-yo. It doesn't work unless you do. And in winding that (values) string, you inspect every inch of it. You clean every inch of it and you get every inch of performance out of it."*

And loving leaders even celebrate that creative tool every day just like that new CEO does: working at a desk flanked by so many yo-yos. Strings attached. By design. With conviction!

Mint 63

MAKING LOVE
In The Checkout Lane

Today's EngageMINT
*Embrace a compelling feeling that
celebrates something bigger than you.*

Methodically and precisely the former fighter pilot in World War II steered his grocery-cart scooter into the checkout lane. He grimaced as he gripped the soup can in his cart. The pain shot through his frail 85-year-old hand like so many bullets. Wincing, he dropped the can of soup on the conveyor belt with a thud! The sound caught the attention of the customer in front of him. The 40-year-old abruptly turned his attention from the cashier scanning his groceries to the elderly man behind him. The younger man seemed captivated both by the cap the octogenarian wore and the compelling message it bore: ***WWII Veteran***.

Something stirred deep in the soul of the younger man. Something seared deep into his memory. He felt a sudden urge that he could no longer contain. Intuitively or—instinctively more than impulsively—the younger man thrust his hand out almost as if he were to salute the Veteran. But then he paused, grabbed the hand of the frail man and shook it earnestly. He looked deep into the eyes of the man old enough to be his grandfather and beamed with as much patriotism as pride: "Thank you for your service to our country."

The Veteran smiled when he found his feeble hand engulfed in the younger man's grip. Suddenly the cold shot of pain in his hand dissipated in the soothing warmth of the younger man's hand. And for at least a few seconds the World War II Veteran felt the burden easing on his heart of so many painful memories of so many dear friends lost in their collective quest to stand up for their country. The two men seemed so different, so rooted in their deep generational divide and so far apart in their lifestyles. Yet in this moment, in this place, they became one. In those few seconds another human—a stranger no less—had recognized and rewarded him for his valor and values and literally reached out to him. And together in this most ordinary place doing the most ordinary thing they made love in a business context. They appreciated each other. They regarded each other. They added value to each other. They shared a common belief, a common passion, a common purpose and a shared conviction. And then it was over. The old man continued to painfully grip his soup cans onto the conveyor belt. The younger man completed his purchase with the cashier. The older man was now just another customer in front of the cashier. But for an instant, the cashier witnessed how love in a business context can happen anywhere two or more people focus their attention on someone or something bigger than either of them without any pending agenda or expectation of a reciprocal action.

So the next time you're feeling depressed, look for love in the checkout lane at your nearest Big Box Store. Forget Retail Therapy. Spend time more than just money in the checkout lane and you just might transform that lane into a quasi "lovers lane." That's not as over-the-top as it sounds. Consider the elderly lady who searched frantically through her purse looking for that $50 bill she was sure was there. But it wasn't. She told the cashier to take back the $46 worth of groceries he had just scanned. The customer behind felt compelled to help: "Just put those remaining groceries on my bill. I will pay for that," she told the cashier.

The elderly lady sighed in relief and blurted "Bless you." The cashier thought the two were related the way they were chatting a few minutes before about the clothes the older customer was buying for her grandchild. Later the cashier discovered the two customers did not know each other before their spontaneous meeting triggered an appreciation for something bigger than each of them: caring and sharing for others who care and share for others. With conviction!

Mint 64

Climbing Down
From Your Ivory Tower

●

Today's EngageMINT
Stay in touch with the rank and file.

Executives can easily be insulated and maybe even isolated from the average employee's world. High-powered executives daily are ensconced in chauffeured limousines, protected from the real world's traffic and congestion. They live in spectacular homes in gated communities protected from the real world of crime and grime. These high-powered executives work in palatial offices with breath-taking views. They rule from on high—high above the real work-a-day world of life for so many millions of people who are confined to a cubicle or sentenced to operate a machine for eight hours a day. There are no house keepers, nannies, chefs, or gardeners in the average employee's world.

Gaining Access

That's why a supervisor in a manufacturing plant was pleasantly surprised when he learned the president of their billion-dollar global company lived in a middle class neighborhood not far from the corporate headquarters and nowhere near a gated community. The company president drove himself to work in his midsized car. And on any given Saturday afternoon the company president could be found at home mowing his own lawn.

Why did this millionaire choose to live more like one of his average employees than like most other company presidents? Access. "All employees need to know they can talk to THEIR company president any time they need to," the company president explained. The president taught a valuable lesson to all leaders: climb down from your ivory tower and get as close as possible to your front-line employees. Then you will learn what is really going on in your company with greater detail and documentation than a status report written days or weeks later. Of course the president already had a well utilized Open Door Policy at his company. But this president opened his door even wider. And in the process, the president leveraged his understanding and appreciation for what average employee lives were like—on and off—the job. His sense of personal humility and vulnerability—no gated community and no chauffer—engendered a working environment of mutual trust in the employee profit-sharing private company.

That trust between employees and management has been instrumental in the company operating for more than 100 years without a union and without any employee strikes. "Without employees who feel valued, you don't have a company, you have an organization," the president said. And the difference between an organization and a company? People. A company, rooted around people—and anchored only by their creative zeal — grows over time because of its ever-surging synergy. Meanwhile an organization, rooted around processes and systems—and anchored only by its weakest link—slows in time because of its ever-draining energy.

Company For Dinner

It's instructive that we focus on people when we say that we are having company over for dinner. The word company stems from the Latin word for bread (panis). So the most enlightened leaders—virtually and literally—break bread with their employees. Together they build a mutually beneficial relationship that nets a productive and profitable company. Of course there are all kinds of security issues today that would undermine this wide of a wide open Open Door Policy. But the concept of climbing down out of your Ivory Tower to get a real feel for the real world is still viable. What can you do to become even more accessible and approachable to your employees? Consider these six ideas to get you even closer to your people and to your company:

1. **HOBBY SHOWCASE:**

Invite all employees to showcase their hobbies in the cafeteria. Have a day dedicated to Pottery or Model Airplane hobbyists etc. Stage an all-afternoon barbeque. Invite C-Suite leaders to take a shift barbequing and grilling for their employees. Invite leaders of the company to visit the exhibits and talk to employees during their lunch hours or before or after shifts so that production will not be affected.

2. **COFFEE WAGON:**

Tour the manufacturing plants in a golf cart toting hot coffee and donuts. Serve the coffee and donuts at key stops just before the work day begins. Beware: You might have to get up at 4 am just like some of your employees.

3. **RANDOM LUNCHES:**

Invite 6-8 employees at random for lunch with the president of the company. (Perhaps those who share the same birthdate or birth month).

4- RELOCATE EMPLOYEE SNACK ROOM:

Consider converting your main reception desk into a free snack bar for customers, employees, and management to interact.

5-CREATE A CORPORATE CAMPFIRE:

Place a coffee urn in the middle of your most populated work area (attracting workers from next floor up or down) for a specific period each day and the coffee won't be the only thing brewing. Workers in sight often give leaders an insight.

6. FORM A CREATIVITY EXPLORERS GROUP:

Invite all employees to informal brown bag lunches to discuss ideas on creativity.

Together these different employees from different departments become much like the different grapes from different vineyards in a Dom Perignon bottle of champagne. They interact together in a second fermenting process. They catalyze each other with an enriching sense of synergy that brings out the best in each other. And they break down the insulation—and often the isolation—of the C-Suite. With conviction.

Mint 65

SYNERGY
Leading Meetings Like a Trapeze Artist

Today's EngageMINT
Seek an interchange
of ideas with your staff.

Swinging and soaring 80 feet high over the arena floor, the trapeze artists exhibited enormous trust in each other, one letting go of the swing to fly into the life-saving catch of the other acrobat. Together they accelerated their aerial defiance of the laws of physics. Then with a third empty swing swinging toward them, they collectively generated so much synergy that one acrobat let go of her swing. But instead of falling, she snared the on-coming empty swing at just the right time with enough momentum as she flew through the air and "landed" 3-5 feet higher. How is that even possible? How do you defy gravity to fly higher?

Loving leaders know.

They understand the power of collective momentum built on trust. They know that carefully crafted momentum stems from a synergy that enhances performance. Marshaling that momentum, the leader and their direct report achieve more working together—interdependently—than they could working independently. That's why the most effective leaders conduct their one-on-one meetings with their direct reports as if they were trapeze artists seeking a greater momentum.

Together they foster a shared grip on the issues and a collaborative spirit of sharing and caring that turns their one-on-one meetings into <u>Fierce Conversations</u> "where there is neither a struggle for approval nor an attempt to persuade," according to Susan Scott in her book *Fierce Conversations*. "There is, instead, an interchange of ideas and sentiments during which you pay attention to and disclose your inner thoughts while actively inviting the other to do the same." In fostering this interchange of ideas the most effective leaders seek first to understand before making themselves understood as Stephen Covey noted in his book *The 7 Habits of Highly Effective People.*

Focusing On Intent
As Much As Content

They listen with feeling for feelings. They focus on THE intent as much as THE content. And they anchor their Fierce Conversations—their one-on-one meetings—around an interchange of ideas more than simply an exchange of project updates, budget approvals and to-do lists.

In sparking this interchange of ideas, the leader and his or her direct report weave a tapestry of new ideas and new relationships that heightens their reach—like the trapeze artists— way out of their comfort zone: as much up and down the organization as across the breadth of the organization. And together they guard against the human tendency to fall back into their comfort zone and focus more narrowly in their own backyard—only on their patch—in the patch-work quilt of the organization.

After all, veteran weavers will tell you that weaving above and beyond your immediate focus is even more difficult when you consider the up-and-down weaving process (warp) is hidden beneath the side-to-side weaving process (weft). However it is the vertical warp—acting much like a trapeze swing—that provides the inner strength to the fabric, an inner strength that fosters a sense of synergy that keeps the threads of the organization aligned and the leader's Fierce Conversations refined. With conviction!

Mint 66

INTEGRITY
When No One Is Looking

●

Today's EngageMINT
*Someone is always
watching you: You.*

Diligently, a Greek sculptor carved the back of a statue's head. No matter that virtually no one would ever see his handiwork especially on the 40-foot tall statue placed against a wall inside the Parthenon in Athens. A bystander chided Phidias for working so hard on the back of his *Athena*: "Who would know?" "I will know," Phidias stated sternly. Leaders always know. No matter who's watching. Or not. That's because leadership is built upon the pillars of integrity. Those pillars remain solid, grounded and anchored no matter how rumbling the landscape or how trembling the road ahead. With integrity leaders remain whole no matter how many ad hoc situations or circumstances tempt them to cut corners. In fact the word integrity stems from the root word "Integer" which is a whole number.

With integrity, leaders remain whole like a hologram no matter how many times that hologram is cut. When you cut a hologram in pieces each piece still retains the whole picture. The whole image remains intact on each of the smaller pieces and each piece can spawn growth.

With integrity, leaders remain whole like a starfish no matter how many times that starfish is cut. When you cut a starfish into pieces any pieces that contain part of its central disc will develop into a new starfish.

With integrity, leaders remain whole like a magnet no matter how many times that magnet is cut. When you cut a magnet in half you magnify rather than weaken its power and you get two equally powerful magnets. Likewise the power of a leader remains whole, fortified with conviction especially whenever his or her integrity is tested. Consider the new car dealer who remained whole when his integrity was tested. He decided not to ask the car manufacturer to replace an engine on warranty. He clearly had the legal right. The engine was still under warranty. His staff fully expected they would bill the manufacturer just like they had always done under the previous management. But then the leader of the dealership learned his own mechanics had inadvertently burned the engine out. And now with his integrity on the line, the loving leader seized the teaching moment. He paid the $650 replacement cost. He admitted his dealership was at fault. The leader of the dealership sent a clear message: act with integrity in your business dealings. He noted: "If you will steal from someone else to benefit me, you will ultimately end up stealing from me."

Another CEO sent a clear message on integrity when he chose to drive his own automobile to the office every day. The CEO parked his car as always in front of his corporate headquarters building. He noticed his left front tire looked flat. Later that morning, he asked his company's fleet garage to fix the leak. They did. The next morning the CEO stopped by to visit the fleet garage with his personal checkbook to pay for fixing the tire on his personal car. The surprised mechanics and technicians in the company's fleet garage got the message loud and clear. No perks. No free lunches.

The CEO knew his $22 check to fix a tire would ultimately earn the company thousands of dollars in more efficient use of parts and materials, especially as word spread in the privately held, employee profit-sharing company. In paying with his personal check, he paved the way for many future loving leaders to emerge. He wanted a paper trail to tell and retell his story of his integrity. The CEO later explained: "If you want to lead others, you've got to have their trust, and you can't have their trust without integrity." And loving leaders realize that you can't have integrity without a finely tuned moral compass consistently pointing you to your TRUE north (or pointing you toward the back of a Greek statue's head). With conviction!

Mint 67

Amor Vincit Omnia
(Love Conquers All)
Even Failure

Today's EngageMINT
*Failures: Endear 'em
more than endure 'em.*

Failure isn't for failures. It's for leaders who realize that failure is part and parcel of success. You can't have one without the other. Success comes BECAUSE OF—not in spite of—failure. Rowland Macy founded the Macy's department store in 1858 after failing at seven previous attempts to open a dry goods store. Louis Meyer founded MGM in 1924 from three failed companies including one failed company of his own. And Henry Ford built his first car 15 years after he failed at building a mechanical plow. Ford said: "Failure is not failure, but the opportunity to begin again, more intelligently." Abraham Lincoln failed eight times to win elected office before becoming President of the United States. And Thomas Edison persisted through 12,000 failures before finding the right filament to invent the light bulb.

Leaders understand that failure refines and refocuses your conviction. That's why leaders convene every year for a conference dedicated to learning from failure, a conference where the participants subscribe to the premise that FAIL is an acrostic that means First Attempt In Learning. That conference is called FailCon where leaders gather to study "their own and others' failures and prepare for success."

No wonder failure isn't for failures. Failure gives you another chance to take another more educated shot; to review and revise what you have done so you can do it better the next time and to realize that failure is the condiment that gives success its flavor as author Truman Capote observed. "If you want to succeed, double your failure rate," noted Tom Watson, founder of IBM. Leaders know only too well that the fear of failure keeps them on their toes and in good fighting condition. In the movie *The Great Santini* the fighter pilot's son asks his dad if he is afraid when he flies. The fighter pilot replies: "Hell, yeah, that's what makes me such a great pilot."

Fear Stimulates Growth

That's why loving leaders make failure and the fear of failure work for them. In fact without fear, we would not be able to grow observes Joshua Liebman in his book *Peace of Mind* "since fear is often the stimulus." Fear is often the stimulus that forces emerging leaders out of their protective cocoons to confront new challenges and uncover new opportunities. In growing from that cocoon into the Butterfly of their Being, the most effective leaders fall in love with what they are doing and their loving feeling sparks a renewed passion to soar higher and higher to cope and conquer their fear. They seek to learn and understand to drive out fear as famed scientist Marie Curie noted: "Nothing in life is to be feared, it is only to be understood. Now is the time to understand more so that we may fear less."

That's why loving leaders fully embrace the literal meaning of the word fear: from the Old English word (Faran) which means "to go." So fear in general and failure in particular serve as a catalyst for an action-oriented initiative to grow leaders "to go"—especially those committed to on-going learning and loving where *Amor vincit omnia* (love conquers all). Even failure. As motivational guru Tony Robbins, observes: "If people will lead with love and caring, they will find a way. But if they lead with their fear they will fail."

In leading with love and caring, the most effective leaders stir their imagination and ignite their engines to persist and to perform at optimum levels, no matter how rugged the road or how many fears and failures en route. As loving leaders they are geared "to go." With conviction!

Mint 68

Turning Mistakes Into Learning Moments

●

Today's EngageMINT
Mistakes = new paths to continuous improvement.

So you made a mistake and now you're feeling bad. Well cheer up! If misery loves company, you've got plenty of company in the mistake department. Even Albert Einstein, Thomas Edison and Aristotle made snap judgements that were less than buttoned down:

- **Albert Einstein** said in 1932—13 years before the advent of nuclear energy—that there is not the slightest indication that nuclear energy will be obtainable. *Oops!*
- **Thomas Edison** said that no one would ever use alternating current. *Oops!*
- **Aristotle** said it was absurd to think that wind was really air in motion. *Oops!*

The most effective leaders make mistakes. If you weren't making mistakes, you wouldn't be leading the new and different. You would be following the proven and sound. That's why loving leaders see mistakes as learning opportunities to keep them vigilant in the marketplace, according to Garry Ridge, the CEO at The WD-40 Company. He calls mistakes *Learning Moments* that focus on a shared responsibility toward continuous improvement. That's why the most effective leaders don't play the blame game when things go awry. They bring their A-game and start again to solve the problem from an alternative direction based on their *Learning Moment*. Mistakes are like stepping stones that help you cross the creek flowing with the currents of experimenting, learning and understanding. Maybe that's why Edward Land, then president of Polaroid, had a plaque in his office that read: "A mistake is an event, the full benefit of which has not yet been turned to your advantage." In fact, mistakes can open the door to new understandings of self awareness that enhance your overall performance in the future, notes psychologist Lisbeth Sunders Medlock. In a column for Huffington Post, Medlock opined:

> "**1. Mistakes teach us to clarify what we really want and how we want to live.** The word mistake derives meaning only by comparison to what we desire, what we see as success. Noticing and admitting our mistakes helps us get in touch with our commitments—what we really want to be, do, and have. Mistakes wake us up and focus our attention like a flashing sign that says "fix this." The urgency created causes us to focus on issues or problems that make us feel off track. Working on possible solutions, redefining what we want or expect, or reexamining our values or goals can lead us to more clarity about our path.

> "**2. Mistakes teach us about ourselves and how to tell our truth.** It is natural to want to cover up our mistakes or be embarrassed by them. To feel like we wish we had a handy mistake eraser or remover. But being honest about our failures and limitations offer us opportunities to practice telling the truth. Admitting the truth allows us to expand our knowledge of self-to know who we are. And thus, increases our capacity to change. It is like holding up a mirror to ourselves and really seeing. When we tell others about our mistakes, to let them really see us, it allows us to let go of the embarrassment, shame and blame we may feel so that we can concentrate on learning and growing.

> "**3. Mistakes teach us to accept our fallibility and face our fear.** Sometimes even our best efforts just don't work out. We might do everything possible to achieve a certain result and still fail, again and again. When this happens we can admit that we're stuck. Facing mistakes often takes

us straight to the heart of our fears. And when we experience and face those fears, they can disappear. When we are stuck and admit that we can't do it alone it sends a signal and opens the door for help to show up. People, resources, and solutions will appear, especially when we ask for help."

In asking for help, leaders realize the learning opportunity their mistake gives them. They see their mistake is actually a mis-step on the walkway of success. They come to understand their mistake more as a "miss-take" in the movie of their lives. Hollywood movie directors think of a "take" as the uninterrupted filming of a scene and a "miss" is something off target. So a miss-take—or a mistake—is an off-target scene. Leaders simply refocus. They get a new view and they begin anew, turning their missteps into more precise next steps, more focused Learning Moments.

And significantly they stay forward leaning and reaffirm their continuous improvement mindset. No woe is me! No pity partying. The most effective leaders see their mistakes as so many mile markers on the road to success. The more mistakes the closer they are to reaching their success. Loving leaders share the thinking of Benjamin Franklin when the famed inventor and statesman noted: "The man who does things makes many mistakes but he never makes the biggest mistake of all—doing nothing."

The Biggest Mistake: Not Making Mistakes

Doing something–even making a mistake—can be a blessing in disguise as Chinese philosopher Wang Yang-Ming notes: "The sages do not consider that making no mistakes is a blessing. They believe that the great virtue of man lies in his ability to correct his mistakes and continually to make a new man of himself." That's what loving leaders do. They create a working environment where people "feel safe taking professional risks," notes Robert Siegel Jr. in his book *Learn to Lead With Love* "They are not afraid to make mistakes knowing that you as the leader have their backs." And sometimes those mistakes turn into profitable opportunities. May all your *Learning Moments* be as profitable as these:

Coca-Cola was created by mistake. A fountain clerk in Atlanta mistakenly added soda water instead of tap water to John S. Pemberton's jar of new syrup.

Ivory soap was created by mistake. A factory worker mistakenly left a soap-mixing machine on when he went to lunch. When he returned, he found so much air had been whipped into the soap that it floated.

Lifesavers candy was invented by mistake. A machine used to press mints together malfunctioned and mistakenly pressed too hard on the mints, forming the tiny candy rings.

Wheaties cereal was invented by mistake. A worker mistakenly spilled bran porridge on a hot stove.

Rubber shoes were invented by mistake. Charles Goodyear mistakenly dropped a chunk of sulfur-cured rubber on a hot stove. Instead of melting, the rubber got stronger.

The *Popsicle* was invented by mistake. A lemonade salesman mistakenly left a glass of lemonade with a spoon in it on his windowsill overnight. The lemonade froze.

The *Microwave oven* was invented by mistake. A candy bar mistakenly melted in a worker's pocket from the microwave signals while engineers at Raytheon experimented with the microwave.

And **Shatterproof Safety Glass** was invented by mistake. A French scientist mistakenly knocked over a glass bottle that was coated inside with a transparent chemical (plastic cellulose nitrate) that had evaporated. The bottle fell six feet to a stone floor. The glass cracked but did not break.

Indeed, mistakes are *Learning Moments*. With conviction!

Mint 69

SAFE LANDING
Turning Rejection Into an Ejection

Today's EngageMINT
Think ejected
whenever you're rejected.

Rejected again. You didn't get that job or that promotion. Your last "great" idea bombed. And right now your self-worth is so low you feel about as needed as a pants presser in a nudist colony. What can you do? Try re-framing your experience. Tell yourself you're being EJECTED not rejected.

Think of yourself as if you were a computer disc ejected from the hard drive. Not rejected. Reject implies incompatibility to a given specific situation (i.e. the body rejects a heart). Eject implies versatility in finding a more supportive climate, much like a fighter pilot EJECTS when his plane is damaged.

That's why leaders facing rejection think of themselves as an ejected pilot. They know they will eventually land safely in an environment where they can thrive more than merely survive. The most effective leaders routinely see rejection as part of the business process. As every sales person knows, getting someone to say "yes" means first getting 10 or more who say "no."

Leaders don't take rejection personally. They simply move on to greener pastures and brighter days like this: Albert Einstein's dissertation was rejected at the University of Berlin for being "irrelevant and fanciful." He brushed off that rejection and discovered the Theory of Relativity. Walt Disney's application for employment as a cartoonist at the Chicago Tribune and the Kansas City Star was rejected. He brushed off that rejection and founded Disneyland and Disney World. As a teenager Winston Churchill got a report card from his teacher regarding his "conspicuous lack of success." He brushed off that rejection and eventually became the Prime Minister who led Great Britain to her finest hour. The television series, *M*A*S*H* was initially rejected by 32 producers. The creators brushed off that rejection and *M*A*S*H* went on to become the top-ranked program by *TV GUIDE* magazine in the first 40 years of television's history.

Rejection is an integral part of the publishing process. That's why the most successful authors reject their rejection and eventually eject themselves into a more welcoming land of readers for their books.

Consider that:

- Mystery writer John Creasey collected 743 rejection slips before publishing 564 books.
- Playwright Rod Serling, creator of television's iconic *The Twilight Zone,* wrote 40 manuscripts before selling his first one.
- Theodore Geisel's first Dr. Seuss book was rejected 23 times.
- Walt Whitman's most famous book of poems –*Leaves of Grass*—was rejected so often, he ended up self-publishing it.
- Jules Verne's first novel *Five Weeks in a Balloon* was rejected four times. He went on to write 62 books.

Chances are that none of those famous authors thought of themselves as being rejected. Instead they may well have thought of themselves as being ejected and landing safely in a new more supportive working environment. Now they could pursue their passion with the renewed conviction of a Viktor Frankl who wrote *Man's Search for Meaning* in nine days; with the renewed conviction of a Wayne Dyer who wrote *Your Erroneous Zones* in 18 days and with the renewed conviction of a Voltaire who wrote *Candide* in four weeks. And so the leadership lesson is clear: loving leaders turn their rejection slips into ejection clips and land with an even greater sense of passion and purpose. With conviction!

Mint 70

FRICTION
Bringing Out The Shine Over Time

Today's EngageMINT
Press on when the pressure is on.

With a machine-gun like rhythm – rat-a-tat, rat-a-tat, rat-a-tat– the skilled shoe shine entrepreneur attacked the pair of leather shoes so fervently they squealed under the siege of his polishing cloth. Those shoes took a beating and came out beaming. Just like a leader.

Next time you feel the friction in the marketplace, the next time you feel someone is trying to rub you out, take a look at the shine on your shoes. Put a smile on your face and appreciate the value of friction. Leaders know that friction can rev you up not just wear you down, especially in quest of a labor of love.

Consider the beating that Don Shula took in becoming the first pro football coach to lose two Super Bowls in embarrassing fashion. Nevertheless, with his shoes figuratively beaten beneath all of that friction, Shula battled back to outshine the competition the next year. He coached the 1972 Miami Dolphins to the first unbeaten, untied 17-0-record in more than a half century of the National Football League and went on to win Super Bowl VII.

Beaten, battered and bruised, the Miami Dolphins battled back stronger than ever before for a perfect record that still stands today nearly a half century later. But the friction that Shula faced over those three years before finally shining at the Super Bowl was fierce. In the 1969 season, his Baltimore Colts took a beating in the Super Bowl. Baltimore lost to Joe Namath and the underdog New York Jets in one of sport's all-time upsets, 16-7, in Super Bowl III. Then in the 1971 season, Shula's Miami Dolphins set the Super Bowl record for scoring the fewest points and for logging the most time to be shutout in a game before finally scoring with 3:19 remaining in its 24-3 loss in Super Bowl VI to the Dallas Cowboys. But the Dolphins bounced back with a shine over time.

Playing their way from the outhouse to the penthouse in 12 months, the scuffed Dolphins emerged like a new pair of shined shoes. They took a beating and got bolder and better, stronger and more resilient. They became much like pulp in the manufacture of fine paper. The more the pulp is beaten with revolving iron bars the finer the paper. Press on when the pressure is on.

That's what passionate and purposeful leaders do. The next time you feel pressed for time or under pressure from competitors, think of yourself as if you were like so many sweet herbs that give their fragrance best when pressed over and over again. Parlay that pressure the way coal turns to diamonds when pressed over time Take some solace in knowing that the strongest steel is forged in the hottest fire. And realize "A gem cannot be polished without friction nor man perfected without trials,"as the Chinese proverb says.

No gem can be polished without friction

Leaders leverage friction. They realize that friction can spark a new insight from a different perspective. Consider the way Richard Nixon paid tribute to friction in his political life when he was forced to resign in disgrace as the President of the United States in 1974. Writing in his book *In the Arena*, Nixon recalled viewing the Grand Canyon in all its splendor for the first time. He hiked seven miles down and looked up to see an even greater splendor and feel an even more enriching insight. "Only when you have been in the depths can you truly appreciate the heights," Nixon observed, echoing the wit who said: "A tea kettle sings best when it's up to its neck in hot water." Friction sparks a leader's convictions, beliefs, values in the crucible of their passionate persistence. Even in the face of a nightmare. Consider this scenario:

You're driving on a two-lane highway in the pre-dawn darkness. Suddenly you see four headlights beaming abreast of each other and heading directly towards you.

As you get closer, you see that the four headlights belong to a Greyhound bus and a truck. The bus is trying to pass the truck when suddenly the hand of death SLAPS you hard! Painfully hard.

You lie torn, twisted and tangled in a head-on collision with the Greyhound bus. You lie helpless, hapless and hopeless in your prison of personal pain. You lie virtually paralyzed—a whisper away from death's door—for four months.

Suddenly, incredibly and miraculously, you recover. And just over a year later, you win one of the most prestigious and competitive sporting events in history.

Sound farfetched? Who could defy death like that? Who could defy the odds like that? Who could defy destiny like that?

Golf great Ben Hogan—that's who.

In 1950, just 16 months after his head-on collision with a bus, Ben Hogan amazed the sporting world with his stunning comeback.

He won the US Open in a strenuous 36-hole playoff, proving once again that friction can bring out the shine over time.

That's why loving leaders press on when the pressure is on even in the aftermath of a physical disability. Consider these examples of human motivation and conviction:

Samuel Johnson blind in one eye, nevertheless spent nine years writing the first modern English dictionary.

John Trumbull who had only one eye created historic paintings including the Declaration of Independence.

Louis Pasteur, his left leg and arm paralyzed, discovered the cure for rabies.

Franklin Delano Roosevelt, stricken with polio at age 39, became the only president of the United States elected to four consecutive terms.

Itzhak Perlman, paralyzed with polio at the age of four, became a famous violinist.

Winston Churchill, born with a speech defect, became one of the world's greatest orators and prime minister of England during World War II.

Meanwhile a quick check of the sports history books shows that: *Tom Dempsey*, born without most of his right foot, still kicked his way into the National Football League's record books for 43 years with the longest field goal (63 yards). And *Jim Abbott*, born without a right hand, still pitched major league baseball for 10 years and struck out 888 batters.

Other leaders learned how to press on when the pressure was on. Consider *Helen Keller*. As a two-year-old, Helen lost her sight and hearing. By age seven, Helen could not see, hear or speak. But by age 25, Helen Keller spoke English, French and German. She read Latin and Greek and she graduated with honors from Radcliffe College (in four years). Still blind and deaf, Helen Keller became the first woman to earn at honorary degree at Harvard University. She went on to write 12 books and became an accomplished public speaker for nearly 50 years. Indeed loving leaders realize that with adversity can come exemplary performance. Friction brings out the shine in the most effective leaders. With conviction!

Mint 71

Taking CARE of Business

Today's EngageMINT
*Be respectful & resourceful
in soothing tempers.*

Ping! The cash register drawer sprang open with a vigor ready for business and the cashier's jaws dropped open in dismay at a checkout lane in the busy Big Box store. Whoa! What happened here? The cashier, who just relieved the previous cashier, needed 86 cents change back to complete the sale with her first customer. She didn't have 86 cents in the drawer. This was the first time in her three years that cashier protocol had been so severely abridged. The previous cashier didn't order more change as is customary before turning over her cash register to her relief for the day. Exasperated, the cashier slammed the cash register closed, punched a few numbers into the machine to order the necessary cash and coins and then summoned her supervisor over to help resolve the situation.

The cashier was so upset over the embarrassing situation in front of the customer that she could hardly speak when the supervisor arrived. The cashier thought it better to show her supervisor the problem instead of try to explain it. She asked the supervisor to use her management key to manually open her cash drawer. The supervisor opened the cash drawer, saw the dearth of coins and bills, looked at the forlorn cashier and matter-of-factly said: "So? Order more change." "I did. That's not the problem here," the cashier shot back. "This is a training issue. I can't do my job unless you do your job. Train these new people." The supervisor passed the blame on to "personnel who sent us six new cashiers to train at the same time." That blame game made the cashier even more frustrated and her supervisor even more infuriated. In the end the company lost the full services of a highly rated cashier for the rest of that day and for many days that followed. After all, she felt that if her bosses did not care about her needs to help her serve her customers, why should she care? But loving leaders do care, especially in resolving conflict situations like this where a valued employee is miffed because of a preventable mistake. That's why the most effective leaders follow the **CARE** model of conflict management. Let's apply the **CARE** acrostic to this no-cash-in-the-cash- register scenario:

CONCERN:

If the employee is concerned, the supervisor shares that same concern—at least initially. The supervisor would have had a better outcome if she paused, looked the cashier in the eyes and then asked in a soft and friendly supportive manner, "How can I help?" Then while listening to the cashier vent the supervisor complies to the cashier's request to open the cash drawer.

AFFIRM:

Then as soon as the supervisor saw the lack of cash and coins in the cash register, the supervisor would have had a better outcome by affirming the cashier's perception of the situation: that the cashier could not serve her customers without an adequate supply of cash and coins in the register and secondly that this obviously preventable mistake embarrassed her in front of her customers.

RESOLVE:

Then the supervisor would have had a better outcome by making sure the change the cashier had ordered earlier was en route and making sure that training new cashiers in proper cashier protocol would be reinforced rather than blaming others and citing excuses.

ENGAGE:

Then both the supervisor and the cashier would have had a better outcome going forward if the supervisor had commiserated with the cashier's frustration, vowed to fix the training issue once and for all and more fully recognized and engaged the cashier as a valued employee. With conviction!

Mint 72

BOUNCING BACK
From a Tough Start

Today's EngageMINT
*Battle back from
beleaguered beginnings.*

You got off on the wrong foot. You stumbled out of the block. Now you're sure your project is doomed. Well cheer up! The most effective leaders battle back from tough starts. They stub their toe and get back up and go. With conviction. They're so committed to what they do, so in love with doing it 24/7, that they're driven to bounce back from what others would consider disaster at worse or an embarrassment in the least. Consider that:

PABLO PICASSO, the 20th century's most innovative artist was born dead. His uncle—a physician—tried an innovative approach (breathing cigar smoke into the baby's nostrils to shock the newborn's lungs) and revived him.

JACK NICKLAUS, the greatest professional golfer of all time, took his first swing as a professional golfer and hit his drive into the water. From that disastrous opening at a pro exhibition match in Miami, Nicklaus went on to win a record 18 major tournaments. That's two more major tournament victories than the combined total of Arnold Palmer (7) and Gary Player (9), three times as many as Lee Trevino (6), and four more major tournament victories than Tiger Woods (14). Meanwhile leaders in other sports had tough starts:

WILLIE MAYS, major league baseball's Hall of Fame slugger batted 0 for 5 in his first major league baseball game and collected only one hit in his first 25 trips to the plate. He would go on to hit 660 home runs and play in 24 All Star Games.

JOHN WOODEN, the legendary collegiate basketball coach who won seven consecutive national championships at the University of California at Los Angeles (UCLA) coached his first basketball team to a losing 6-11 season in high school. He went on to coach 12 NCAA college basketball national championship teams.

OSCAR ROBERTSON, the Hall of Fame basketball pro missed his first shot as a college player—an easy layup— playing for the first time in New York City's Madison Square Garden. But then he bounced back that night to score a Garden record 56 points in pacing his University of Cincinnati team to a victory over Seton Hall (scoring more points himself than the entire rival team). Robertson was voted one of the Greatest 50 Players in NBA history and a 12-time NBA All Star.

And **LOU GEHRIG,** the Hall of Fame baseball pro struck out on three straight pitches in his first at-bat in the major leagues. Yet Gehrig went on to set 45 major league baseball records primarily for hitting, including 23 grand slam home runs. He also was the first in the American league to hit four home runs in a single game.

Loving leaders always get up and get going no matter how often they stumble. Imagine, you're missing your right eye and your right arm. You're also suffering from gout, recurring attacks of malaria, chest and lung pains, rheumatic fever and mental depression. Yet, despite all that personal mayhem, British Admiral **HORATIO NELSON** defeated Napoleon's French Navy on October 21, 1805 at the Battle of Trafalgar before falling mortally wounded. "I have done my duty," he said. Even a bullet in the shoulder didn't stop **TEDDY ROOSEVELT** during the 1912 presidential campaign. Roosevelt pulled the blood-soaked manuscript from his pocket that blunted the impact of the bullet and said: "I have a message to deliver as long as there is life in my body." He then delivered his speech as scheduled.

Loving leaders bounce back from tough starts. With conviction!

Mint 73

DANCING
To The Ever-Changing Music

Today's EngageMINT
*Change = catalyst
for continuous improvement.*

When escalators were first installed in department stores, nurses were stationed at the top to tend to those who thought they would feel light headed. When the first air balloon landed after a 15-mile flight in France, the people in the town of 20,000 were so frightened of the air-borne monster they called it "inhuman" and destroyed it with stones and knives. And when the bath tub was introduced in the United States in 1842, it was labeled "a menace to health." Three years later bathing was unlawful in Boston except when prescribed by a physician.

Only vending machines and babies welcome change. "Change imposed is changed opposed," as author Spencer Johnson writes in his book *Who Moved My Cheese*. No wonder Nicolo Machiavelli said: "There is nothing more difficult to take in hand, more perilous to conduct or more uncertain of its success than to take the lead in the introduction of a new order of things." Yet, the most effective leaders are committed to a new order of things. Change agents (leaders) reflect the spirit of innovation and freedom in the gilt letters inscribed above the doors inside the United States Senate chamber: *Novus Ordo Seclorum* "a new order of the ages is born." They recognize and realize that change can regenerate, renovate and rejuvenate like this:

Change Regenerates: More than 98 percent of all atoms in the human body are replaced – changed—in less than one year, says Dr. Deepak Chopra in his book <u>Ageless Body, Timeless Mind.</u> In fact, humans change their outer skin completely every 27 days. **Change Renovates:** Farmers nourish their land with change. They rotate their crops. The soil needs to be refreshed with new nutrients. Likewise tree farmers nourish their land with change. They clear their land every 40 years to give birth to new trees. And **Change Rejuvenates**: Nathaniel Hawthorne, the author, once observed: "Human nature will not flourish if it is planted and replanted in the same worn out soil.

Yet the status quo can dig in its heels in that worn out soil. Resisting change can be so profound that when Russian composer, conductor Igor Stravinsky first presented his ballet *Rite of Spring*, his audience rioted. Resisting change can be so profound that when Claude Monet first exhibited his impressionistic art, people considered it "messy." One newspaper reported that after seeing the Monet, the visitor "went mad, rushed out in the street and started biting innocent passersby."

Nothing is Forever

However, loving leaders learn how to dance to the ever-changing music. They crash through that wall of resistance to new learnings and changing behaviors. They summon their personal and professional conviction. They embrace the insight of Abraham Lincoln who said: "The dogmas of the quiet past are inadequate for the storming present and future. As our circumstances are new, we must think anew and act anew." Nothing is forever. Even Niagara Falls stopped flowing for 30 hours beginning on March 29, 1848 when ice jammed up the river.

Nothing is forever. Today the Nile Valley has no big game and the Sinai is a dry desert. Yet the walls of Egyptian Tombs are covered with hunting scenes of the pharaohs spearing lions or big game. Nothing is forever. Just ask Thomas Friedman who recalls in his 2016 book *Thank You For Being Late* when 4G was a parking space, applications were what you sent to gain college admission, the Cloud was still in the sky, and Twitter used be just a sound. Nothing is forever. That's why the most effective leaders pay their respects to change. And treating change with RESPECT is highly instructive when you consider that the Latin root of the word—Respect (*re-spectare*) —means "to see again." Change is always poised to knock on your door. In paying their respects to change, the most effective leaders even erect monuments to never forget and continually learn from that leadership dictum: conditions change and change conditions. Consider the changing conditions the boll weevil manifested in devastating the cotton fields in southeastern Alabama and forcing cotton farms to start growing peanuts and other crops. That change for the better eventually opened the door to greater profitability and prosperity. The Boll Weevil Monument, erected in 1919, still stands prominently in a busy downtown intersection in Enterprise, AL and its message is still relevant: *Beware of Complacency.*

Beware of Complacency

Cotton ruled southeastern Alabama for generations until the Boll Weevil virtually ate away the region's economic heart. That's when farmers in particular and business leaders in general dedicated the 10-foot monument to revere the boll weevil's power to blow the winds of change. The monument features a statue of a woman that resembles the Statue of Liberty. She is holding a 16-inch depiction of a boll-weevil in a gesture of honor—respectfully more than triumphantly— over her head as if to say: "Behold the Boll Weevil and Beware of Complacency Especially in Highly Successful Organizations."

Today, the Boll Weevil Monument still commands attention as a reminder that good times can change suddenly. That's why the most adept leaders adapt, fighting off complacency and capitalizing on change. And that's why the most effective leaders consistently design and develop their own imagined version of the Boll Weevil Monument to not only survive but thrive in tough economic times. Coping with change is the leader's forte. They stay poised no matter how high they soar or how low they fall.

Loving leaders realize the temporal nature of all things. They welcome that sense of impermanence as a call to continuous improvement, a quest for a greater performance the next time. They embrace the notion of construction and destruction of the mandalas, the sacred sand art of the Tibetan lamas. No matter how many hundreds of man hours or millions of grains of sand they invest in creating that art, they always destroy it shortly after finishing it—as if it were a 20,000-piece puzzle dismantled with a flick of the wrist—to show that nothing is permanent. Nothing.

Consider Ozymandias, the once mighty and powerful king whose statue now lies in forgotten ruins in the desert "boundless and bare," in poet Percy Bysshe Shelley testament of the ephemeral nature of all things. Nothing is permanent. Everything changes over time. That's why loving leaders have to be even-keeled no matter how mighty those waves of change. Like dancers, they have to be stable yet flexible. They have to dance to the ever-changing music, knowing that change can either exalt or halt their hopes and dreams. Consider the way James Allen captured this duality of the mind in coping with change in his book *As a Man Thinketh*:

> *Man is made or unmade by himself. In the armory of his thought he forges the weapons by which he destroys himself.*
>
> *He also fashions the thoughts with which he builds for himself heavenly mansions of joy and strength and peace.*
>
> *Man is the master of his thought, the molder of his character. And the maker and shaper of his condition, environment and destiny."*

Indeed, loving leaders face change head on. No matter how high the proverbial escalators; no matter how deep the proverbial bath tubs, no matter how vast the proverbial boll weevils, no matter how breath-taking and magnificent the mandalas or how great and powerful the Kings. They face change with a forward looking, continuous improving, owner leaning mindset to help their employees "reach their full potential and catch them doing something right," as Ken Blanchard and Spencer Johnson write in their book, *The New One Minute Manager*. With conviction.

Mint 74

Preempting The Pity Party

Today's EngageMINT
Keep singin' in the rain
no matter the strain.

Struggling off the 18th green, the two golfers looked for a super computer to add up their scorecard. They both played that lousy. One executive complained about his less than spectacular play. The other leader had another point of view: "Look at this way, on a per stroke basis we both got our money's worth today." They both laughed.

That reframing of an issue or situation is a keen leadership skill. The most effective leaders can find more than the silver lining in the clouds of life. They readily sing and dance through the rain storms of their lives like Gene Kelly wannabees sloshing through the puddles in the movie: *Singin' in the Rain.* In that movie, Kelly was in love and no amount of rain could dampen his spirits nor blunt his convictions. Likewise, the most loving leaders feel that passionate about their customers, their employees, their products and their services. In love, these optimistic leaders see the rainbow while everyone else sees only the rain.

Consider the rainbows that Henry Kaiser saw in the rain as the president of a shipbuilding company in the United States during World War II. A flood had swept away the levee and buried Kaiser's bulldozers and other heavy equipment in a quagmire of mud and machinery. Kaiser's employees were devastated at the loss that turned a would-be ship-building yard into a gigantic mud pie.

But Kaiser quite literally saw things from a different angle. Wading knee-deep in mud, he responded confidently, "I don't see any mud." One of his employees chided Kaiser, saying, "Just look around we are buried in mud." With his conviction well-grounded, Kaiser looked sternly at the employee and helped his followers see in themselves what he could see—the bright star of hope gleaming across the bleak and dreary sky. Kaiser said: "The difference is this: You are looking down and can't see anything but mud, but I am looking up where I can see nothing but sunshine and clear blue sky."

Seeing Rainbows in the Rain

Of course it is too easy to see and feel the rain before seeing the rainbow, too easy to cast aspersions on the new and different. Focusing more on the rainbows than on the rain, loving leaders preempt The Pity Party no matter how drenched they are. They put their own convictions into perspective, knowing only too well that circumstances could always be worse. Even in a flood. Consider that:

- **William Henry Harrison** caught a cold and died 30 days 12 hours and 30 minutes after he became president of the United States in 1841—the shortest presidential administration—in the history of the United States.

- **General George Patton** who dodged enemy bullets in World War II for many years was killed in a car accident when an army truck ran into his limousine on the day before he was to leave Germany for the United States.

- **General Stonewall Jackson** of Civil War fame was accidentally killed by his own soldiers. The history books also tell us that sculptor Auguste Rodin froze to death. Greek Soothsayer Calchas laughed himself to death while choking on a glass of wine. And Galileo, the first man to peer to the heavens through a telescope, died blind.

No wonder the most effective loving leaders don't waste their time focusing on those potholes along life's highway. They don't have time to whistle in the graveyard on their way to a Pity Party. Loving leaders are too busy singing in the rain. With conviction.

Mint 75

HOPE
The First and Last Act of a Leader

Today's EngageMINT
*With hope in the future,
there's more power in the present.*

Roaring like a wild dragon, the fire scorched the building with its blazing breath. Its flaming fingers dug deeply into the building, plucking out the walls, popping out the windows and pulling out the roof supports. Tears flushed the eyes of the owner of the building. The owner wasn't sure if his tears were coming from the smoke in the air or the choking in his heart. His family's business for nearly 80 years burned to ashes. But that fire couldn't burn out the candle of hope that every loving leader lights with conviction when disaster strikes. Just 36 hours later he re-opened for business in make-shift offices. Twenty years later his business tripled its volume and celebrated its 100th anniversary.

Leaders cope with hope. With hope, breaking points become turning points. With hope powering his self-confidence and conviction, Thomas Edison overcame a business disaster when he was 67. Seven of his light bulb factories burned down. He was underinsured. But within two days Edison brought together a team of 1500 people who immediately began building even bigger and better factories. "No one is ever too old to make a fresh start," Edison said. With that optimistic view, you can almost hear Edison reciting the Japanese haiku: *"My barn having burned to the ground, I can see the moon."* That's why the most effective leaders embrace the awesome power in Hope: the only blessing in life that did not escape from Pandora's Box.

Loving leaders know that with hope in the future, there's more power in the present. Loving leaders know that when the Pilgrims sailed to the New World, they did it with hope. When the pioneers settled the West, they did it with hope. And when Americans landed on the moon, they did it with hope. Indeed "Hope is the power that sparks the human will into taking intrepid action" as psychiatrist Dr. Arnold Hutschnecker writes in his book titled *HOPE, The Dynamics of Self-Fulfillment.*

Leaders Keep Hope Alive

Leaders keep hope alive. In fact, leadership author John Gardner says the first and last act of a leader is to *"keep hope alive."* Leaders realize what medical researchers have proven: Without hope the brain can't function. Computer generated pictures of the brain—the neocortex— show that the brain turns off when people "can't anticipate a positive future," according to Mike Maccoby in his book *Why Work*. Without hope, people are damned to hell, according to the message inscribed over Dante's *Gates of Hell*: "Abandon all hope, Ye, who enter here." No wonder the most effective leaders nurture a sense of hope. Consider the ray of hope that beamed from Martin Luther King Jr. when he said:

"We shall hew out of the mountain of despair, a stone of hope."

Hope as the dictionary defines it is looking forward with desire and with belief in possibility. That's why leaders "help transform follower's needs into positive hopes and aspirations" as Pulitzer Prize winning author James MacGregor Burns writes in his book *Leadership*.

Loving leaders know that their power of hope is potent, that "the natural flight of the human mind is not from pleasure to pleasure but from hope to hope," as author Samuel Johnson noted:

Indeed, loving leaders keep hope alive. With conviction.

Mint 76

INSPIRATION

One Step at a Time

●

Today's EngageMINT
*Strive every day with
no finish line ever in sight.*

When 79-year-old Tom told me he was training to run a 26-mile, 385-yard marathon, I laughed. And then about a year later I cried. I cried tears of joy and amazement while I ran with Tom as he finished his marathon. Tom taught me a critical leadership skill: the power of your personal conviction quite literally can motivate you to take action as a loving leader step by step, day in and day out, and help you progress methodically to your finish line. Thanks in part to Tom's inspiration, I had finished my first marathon earlier that afternoon in just over three hours. I was 27 years old, more than a half century younger than Tom who was still out on the course. For the last five and half hours, Tom was persistently walking and slowly running the 26-mile 385-yard course.

"He was smiling.
I was crying."

I went back out on the course and met him at the 25 mile mark. I ran with him the last mile. He was smiling. I was crying. I was crying because Tom had persisted beyond so many obstacles. Beyond illness. Beyond old age. And beyond dire predictions of his own death. Before embarking on his training for the marathon, his doctor gave him six months to live. Tom lived three more years in demonstrating the courage of his convictions and giving us all a lesson in overcoming the odds with the passion and purpose of a loving leader. Tom evaluated his dilemma: Should he stand on the sidelines and wait for Death? Or should he get in the race and attempt to run away from Death—at least for a while? It all began when Tom sought another medical opinion. He found a doctor who said there was an outside chance that if Tom exercised his lungs (walking) he might beat the odds. At least that's what he thought the doctor said. That doctor cautioned that there was still a chance the exercise might also kill him more quickly. Yet Tom chose to focus on the positive much to the chagrin of his family and friends. Everyone wanted to know why he would chance running a 26-mile marathon? Why not focus on a 2.6-mile walk? Tom told me why when I first met him in his luxurious condo in Pompano Beach, Florida furnished in part with two large oxygen bottles in the living room.

Defeated
But Not Destroyed

That's when he told me a leadership principle I would never forget, something that has inspired me ever since. Tom said: "All my life people have been telling me what do to. Now they are telling me how I am going to die. I want to take charge of whatever life I have left." Tom had the conviction of a leader and the passion to take charge and follow through. No matter the heat. No matter the blisters. No matter the barking dogs along the way. Tom reminded me of Santiago, the Old Man in Ernest Hemingway's The *Old Man and the Sea.* The Old Man persistently ventured out on a small boat day after day to fish in the ocean even though he hadn't caught any fish for 84 consecutive days. "Man may be defeated but not destroyed," says Santiago. That's Tom, persisting through illness and the ravages of old age but never destroyed. Tom did not go gentle into that good night as poet Dylan Thomas urged:

> *"Old age should burn and rage*
> *at the close of day. Rage, rage*
> *against the dying of the light."*

Tom raged against the dying light. He unleashed his own two feet and his ever-widening smile mile after mile to the finish line. And for me, watching him cross that finish line was enough to take MY breath away especially when the image of those tall oxygen tanks in Tom's living room flashed through my mind. Loving leaders, centered in their personal conviction, cannot be denied even by Father Time—at least not for a while. Consider the elderly man who boarded a crowded city bus in New York City:

It was standing room only. No problem. The slightly built silver-haired gentleman got a grip on the overhead bar. Then he looked across the way and he made eye contact with a young woman who sprang to her feet.

"Please sir, go ahead and take my seat." She smiled knowing that she had done her good deed for the day.

The old man smiled back at her. Then resolutely he reached up with the other hand and started doing chin ups on the overhead bar.

People throughout the bus began applauding. The young lady sat back down. Leaders don't let circumstances like age get in their way. Maybe that's why famed playwright William Shakespeare observed that:

> **"Some never seem to grow**
> **old. Satisfied yet ever**
> **dissatisfied,**
> **settled yet ever unsettled.**
> **They always enjoy**
> **the best of what is and**
> **are the first to find**
> **the best of what will be."**

(Even on a crowded bus. Or in a marathon.)

With conviction, loving leaders stave off the complacency that poet John Greenleaf Whittier ruefully observed: "Of all the sad words of the tongue and pen, the saddest are these: It might have been." Loving leaders know that complacency starves the soul of recognition, chokes commitment and stifles achievement. Complacency shrouds itself in a blanket that smothers initiative and enterprise with its web of apathy and indifference. With conviction, loving leaders not only stave off complacency they also wrestle the hands of time. That's why:

- At 98, Titian painted a famous work, the *Battle of Lepanto*.
- At 98, Grandma Moses completed 11 paintings.
- At 91, Hulda Crooks became the oldest woman ever to climb to the top of Mount Fuji, the highest mountain in Japan (12,388 feet).
- At 87, Michelangelo completed the Sistine Chapel.
- At 85, Giuseppe Verdi composed *Ave Maria*.
- At 80 Johann Wolfgang Goethe finished *Faust* the tragic play that many scholars consider the greatest work of German literature.

To leaders who love what they do time becomes an investment that consistently generates dividends. There is no end game. No cash out. No time constraint. No planned retirement. No specific date to get off the merry-go-around—only another chance to keep moving, keep doing and keep growing.

That's why Winston Churchill's understanding of time as a continuing investment not a diminishing asset surprised a photographer half his age. As the former Prime Minister who led Great Britain to its finest hour during World War II posed on his 75th birthday, the professional photographer gushed. "I hope that in 25 years I will take your picture on your 100th birthday!" Churchill looked him over slowly and then said: "I don't see why not young man. You look reasonably fit and healthy to me." The photographer grinned as Churchill smirked in the aftermath of sticking his own personal dagger into Father Time. In wrestling the hands of time, loving leaders with a passion and a purpose don't look for a vacant seat on the bus. These seasoned leaders are too busy driving the bus. Or running after the bus. With conviction!

COMPETITION
Loving It Like a Leader

●

Today's EngageMINT
Competitors: catalyst for your success.

Y ou're in a slump. You lost a major account this week. Your competition is bearing down on you. What do you do? Take a deep breath. Applaud your competition. That's what loving leaders do. Take it from Dennis Conner, America's Cup yacht racing winner and the author of the book *The Art of Winning*: "Keep an eye on the competition. Be glad they're tough to beat. Your toughest competitors are your biggest allies in the art of winning. They're the ones who make you work harder, move faster, and think smarter." And they become King or Queen of the Forest as celebrated in this poem on symbiotic power of competition from that prolific author Mr. or Mrs. Anonymous:

The tree that never had to fight,
For sun and sky and air and light

That stood out in the open plain and
Always got its share of rain.

Never became a forest king,
But lived and died a scrubby thing.

Babe Ruth became a forest king in fighting for his sun, sky and air and light while hitting his way into the baseball record books. Ruth relished his competition. He hit a record 60 home runs in 1927 after a season-long duel with teammate Lou Gehrig. As competitors, Ruth and Gehrig showcased the significance of competition: to spark heightened performance in each other. In fact, the word "competition" stems from the Latin phrase *"con petere"* which means "to seek together." With healthy competition a leader's listening is more discerning, a leader's actions are more strategic, and a leader's focus is more productive Without healthy competition you can get too complacent. You can be lulled into thinking you are better than you actually are. "In the country of the blind, the one-eye man is king," noted philosopher Desiderius Erasmus.

Competition affords a reality check that spurs innovation. When escalating competition and ever-changing circumstances seem to flood the Blame and Shame River, the most effective leaders push back with a beaver's bite and dam the flow to grow a more conducive environment. As leaders with a deeply held conviction and a purpose-filled mission, they create their own circumstances the way playwright George Bernard Shaw once asserted:

> *"People are always blaming their circumstances for what they are. I don't believe in circumstances. The people who get on in this world are the people who get up and look for the circumstances they want and if they can't find them, make them."*

As leaders, they make those circumstances with a belief in others that enhances innovation and profitability. As leaders, they make those circumstances with a trust in others that empowers an ever-increasing productivity and continuous improvement. As leaders, they make those circumstances with a commitment to others that bolsters a more robust bottom-line and sparks more creative problem-solving. Significantly the most effective leaders make those circumstances with a trait that is the most lasting and sustains a leader's success over time: **LOVE.***

* James Kouzes and Barry Posner in
The Leadership Challenge

EXECUTIVE SUMMARY

Digesting
Leadership Mints
On the Run

Now that you have savored these 77 Leadership Mints to enhance your bottom line by keeping your employees top of mind, how do you begin incorporating these leadership behaviors in your daily routine? That's what this Executive Summary is all about: a quick way to organize these principles of empathy and emotional intelligence as another tool you can use to increase your team's productivity and profitability through Compassion *(Mints 1-20),* Connection (*Mints 21-56)* and Conviction *(Mints 57-77*). Let's begin with a process that you can use to develop a loving business culture (192-195) that will better align these 77 Leadership Mints so that you can quickly access and apply them. Then we'll address how to sustain (196) and nurture (198) that loving business culture before making the business case for leading with love (199-205).

DEVELOPING
A Loving Business Culture

How do you more readily apply the key learnings in these _77 Leadership Mints_ to develop and strengthen your role as a loving leader? Consider this 3-step process that converts the key learning in each Leadership Mint from a one-sentence summary (called *Today's EngageMINT*) into a more instructive narrative. Then review the corresponding Leadership Mint to learn more detail on that specific behavior. This 3-step process on becoming an even more committed loving leader includes:

1. _Reaching In_ to your heart and soul.
2. _Reaching Down_ to anchor your values and vision.
3. _Reaching Out_ to grow others.

The first step–_Reaching In_ is the most difficult. It takes an open mind to reach into your own heart and soul without some defensive posturing. It takes the courage of your convictions to be transparent and vulnerable.

1. REACHING IN

Humility can fortify your strength in tense situations (*Mint 37).* Learn to become comfortable in your own skin *(Mint 8)* and learn to be even more real to close the deal *(Mint 9).* Beware of walling yourself off from others *(Mint 2).* Step outside of yourself to gain insight into others *(Mint 7).* Know that someone is always watching you *(Mint 66).* Critically evaluate your behavior towards others *(Mint 32).* Become more selfless and less selfish *(Mint 25).* Exercise patience *(Mint 48)* and slow things down *(Mint 49).* Remember where you came from *(Mint 11).* And gain strength from your vulnerability *(Mint 43).*

To get started **Reaching In**: Set aside 15 minutes of silence first thing every morning. Meditate. Sort out what's important vs. what's significant. Then you can more efficiently target your own value system for greater achievement when you begin Reaching Down even deeper in your own heart and soul like this:

2. REACHING DOWN

First focus on your Due-to List (*Mint 36).* Stay connected to your values no matter how far you wander *(Mint 62).* Stay in character regardless of the distractions (*Mint 46).* Stand for something (*Mint 57).* Stimulate performance with high expectations *(Mint 28).* Lead by example *(Mint 34).* Embrace a value that's bigger than you. *(Mint 63).* Realize that trust is built over the long term on the Rock of Relationships (*Mint 26).* Give trust with no quid-pro-quo strings attached (*Mint 27).*

Leverage conflict to enhance performance (*Mint 39).* Respect all regardless of their status (Mint 38), especially those who disrespect you (*Mint 16).* Honor the personal rights of your employees (*Mint 17).* Fully share responsibility and accountability (*Mint 55).*

Change is a catalyst for continuous improvement *(Mint 73).* Competition sharpens your success *(Mint 77).* Battle back from beleaguered beginnings *(Mint 72).* Press on when the pressure is on (*Mint 70).*

Be persistently resourceful in surmounting challenges *(Mint 71).* Stay positive: keep singin' in the rain *(Mint 74).* And when it comes to failures: endear 'em more than endure 'em *(Mint 67).* Think ejected whenever you're rejected *(Mint 69).* Realize that poise under pressure enhances results (*Mint 50).*

Mistakes are new paths to continuous improvement (*Mint 68*).

To get started **Reaching Down:** Write your Personal Declaration of what's important in governing yourself and your team. Develop your own version of "We hold these truths to be inevitable...." And then connect this second step on behaviors to the first step on values and you'll be more adept in Reaching Out to help others like this:

3. REACHING OUT

First demonstrate an interest in the personal lives of your employees (*Mint 23*). Visit your direct reports every day in their workstations for a few minutes even if it is just to say "Good Morning" (*Mint 24*). Acknowledge the initial reality others are facing (*Mint 22*).

Empathize with the feelings of others (*Mint 21*). Adapt to the preferences of others (*Mint 33*). Play the role your audience expects (*Mint 47*). Beware how others see you. (*Mint 40*). Love others to bring out the best in them (*Mint 5*). Mine the hidden value in others (*Mint 1*). Generate synergy through interdependence (*Mint 6*). Infuse others to like themselves when you're around (*Mint 20*). Caring heightens human performance (*Mint 31*). Appreciate others individually the way they prefer (*Mint 33*) with intentional listening (*Mint 4*).

Commit to long-term relationships (*Mint 55*). Shed a tear to help others believe more in themselves (Mint 3). Inspire their performance (*Mint 29*). Preserve their self-confidence (*Mint 12*). Step into the shoes of your employees (*Mint 14*).

Be there in person to celebrate long-term relationships (*Mint 15*). Preserve the dignity of others in tense times (*Mint 30*). Maintain self-esteem in resolving conflict (*Mint 35*). Card your employees with a Hallmark Helper (Mint 19).

Hang proverbial mistletoe in your office *(Mint 18)*. Realize that shining the light on others reflects well on you *(Mint 13)*. Leverage your value in creatively connecting with others *(Mint 56)*. Become a Servant Leader (Mint 42) and generate curiosity to rekindle interest *(Mint 41)*. To get ahead help others get ahead *(Mint 51)*. Lay down a welcome mat for visitors *(Mint 53)*. Be effective not just efficient in using technology *(Mint 52)*. Reward your employees rather than award them *(Mint 54)*. Focus on helping others *(Mint 58)* while serving others always in all ways *(Mint 60)*.

Become a Pen Pal with your new staff or new hires *(Mint 64)*. Seek an interchange of ideas with your staff *(Mint 65)*. Light the flame of hope in the darkness of despair *(Mint 75)*.

Remember that action is the traction to climb Mount Happiness *(Mint 59)*. Never give up and strive with all your might *(Mint 76)* without a finish line in sight. Seek to be the best not the biggest *(Mint 61)*.

To get started **Reaching Out:** Clear your calendar for the first hour of every day. No phone calls. No e-mails. No texting. No meetings. Get out of your office. Visit with your staff individually in their offices or workstations. Take notes. Write down ideas, issues and concerns you hear from your employees. Follow up with a personal response that encourages future engagement.

Thank your employees in person and in writing as often as you can. And always give your employees a fair hearing. "Many people are listened to but few people are truly heard," notes author Leonard Sweet in his book *Summoned to Lead.* "Hearing connects us to that which is unseen and unsaid." Loving leaders in particular hear what is unsaid and unseen with more than their ears or eyes.

They also hear with their hear-t.

SUSTAINING
A Loving Business Culture

Reinforce meaning. That's what loving leaders do in sustaining a culture that influences the attitudes and motivates the behaviors of all stakeholders in an organization. They know that a successful culture "is like a greenhouse where people and ideas can flourish—where everybody in the organization, regardless of rank or role, feels encouraged to speak frankly and openly and is rewarded for sharing ideas about new products, more efficient processes and better ways to serve customers," writes Adam Bryant in his book *Quick and Nimble.* To sustain the continued growth of your organization's loving culture consider these four initiatives:

I. MEMORIALIZE

1. Engrave the names of key leaders into the walls of a conference room. Take a cue from the names of 72 scientists and inventors inscribed around the Eiffel Tower's first-level gallery in bold gilded letters two feet high.

2. Give key leaders an insignia—something they actually wear like a pin or display on their desks or in their offices. For example American pilots who logged more than 100 missions flying night sorties in Vietnam for the 609th Air Command Squadron each wore an insignia patch that said "Nimrod" (for hunter) from the Bible.

3. Name a conference room after the founder of the company or name meeting rooms after company innovators.

4. Invest in a piece of art that best describes the vision or mission of the organization. For example, Egyptian and Roman ships had a swan's head carved at the stern. The swan represented the goddess—Isis—protector of sailors.

II.   DISPLAYS

1.   Japanese restaurants display a cone of salt outside as a sign of good health.

2. A major office furniture manufacturer, helping people work together more effectively, showcased an ant farm in the lobby of its sales showroom in New York City.

III.   SYMBOLISM

If a picture is worth a thousand words then a symbol is worth millions. One leader of a mentoring program gave away colorful electrical connectors—the cap-like piece of plastic–that keep wires in a lamp connected and empowered. Mentors were asked to carry the electrical connector in their pocket or purse for the duration of their mentoring commitment.   Mentors then gave their mentees a similar electrical connector to carry on their person whenever they met. The electrical connector symbolized their synergy in their mutual career development in particular and the organization's capability in general.

IV.   MEETING RITUAL

As part of a regularly scheduled staff meeting, conduct a *5-minute Leadership Mints Break.* It's as easy as 1-2-3:

1. A team member is chosen the week before to lead the 5-Minute Leadership Mints Break at the next team meeting.

2. That designated Leadership Mints Break Leader assigns the MINT (or story out of the 77 available) to be read prior to the next team meeting.

3. At the next team meeting the Leadership Mints Break Leader then leads a discussion on the leadership principle called out in that assigned Mint (or story). Fun option: Pass around a candy dish of wrapped mints while savoring a *Leadership Mint.*

NURTURING
A Loving Business Culture

P atience is critical in nurturing a loving culture. Think of a crock pot not a microwave oven as a metaphor as you develop your loving culture. It takes time to nurture a loving culture where constituents feel appreciated, recognized, stimulated and continuously challenged. It takes time for constituents to sense they have control over their work. It takes time for constituents to be recognized for their achievements in making a difference. And it takes patience to allow one's skills, expertise and character the time to simmer in a proverbial stew of a loving leader's mind-set, disposition and emotional intelligence. Patience is the key in nurturing a loving culture as the Bible says in First Corinthians:

Love is patient, love is kind.
It does not envy.
It does not boast.
It is not proud.
It does not dishonor others.

It is not self-seeking.
It is not easily angered.
It keeps no record of wrongs.

Love does not delight in evil
But rejoices with the truth.

It always protects,
always trusts,
always hopes, and
always perseveres.

EPILOGUE

Making the Business Case For Leading With Love

B oost your bottom line with love. Take it from a CEO with proven results: "The bottom line is best served when leaders lead with love," declares Joel Manby, in his book *Love Works*. As CEO of Herschend Family Entertainment, Corp. Manby's leading with love helped grow the company's operating profit 50% over seven years.

How can you generate that kind of consistent growth on your bottom line? Check out the next 11 pages and you'll find the business case for loving like a leader to achieve greater productivity and profitability including the need for tough love (203) and a clear definition of love in a business context. But first let's remind ourselves of the bottom-line benefits that leaders enjoy in leading with love beginning on the next page.

Cashing In On Love

When you consistently treat your staff with dignity and respect—when you champion their interests and skills, and when you recognize them, encourage them, train them and ask for their input—you protect your bottom line from the mayhem of disengaged workers who cost American business $500 billion a year in lost productivity, according to a Gallup poll. And you pave the way for an infusion of benefits bolstering the bottom line.

Studies document that employees in loving working environments trust more, collaborate more, innovate more and trigger more discretionary performance in themselves and others. Employees, who are loved and appreciated on the job, are less likely to sour co-workers, shun customers and stain the brand with a shoddy attitude and a mediocre performance. But with the spirit of love imbued in a working environment, engaged employees lessen stress, ease personal conflicts, trim turnover, decrease absenteeism, cut safety incidences and reduce shrinkage (theft). Even more significantly engaged employees spark the financial health of the organization.

How strong is the bottom line in well-led companies with loving work environments where employees are engaged? In one 15-year comparison study those companies with loving work environments "outgrew their counterparts (those with a less committed workforce) by a 10 to 1 margin, out-earned them by $111 billion and generated 16 times as much wealth for shareholders," observed Bill Catlette and Richard Hadden, the authors of *Contented Cows Still Give Better Milk.* And so the leadership lesson is clear: the more loved and appreciated your employees, the more productive and profitable their performance.

Defining Love
In a Business Context

Heightened awareness. That's what love is in a business context, notes Barbara Fredrickson, a psychologist at the University of North Carolina at Chapel Hill who has conducted more than 25 years of research on positive emotions. In her book *LOVE 2.0*, Fredrickson notes that when humans are in love, they reach out for something beyond their own "cocoon of self- interest" and become more aware of others. They become more likely to focus on the needs, wants and concerns of others and to see things from another's perspective.

In stepping into the shoes of another, in feeling what they are feeling, loving leaders engage in the "selfless promotion of the growth of others," according to philosopher Milton Mayeroff. In focusing on the "selfless promotion of the growth of others," loving leaders invariably engage their organizations in a more productive more profitable relationship, including recruiting and retaining more talented employees, engaging others in more creative and innovative problem solving, reducing government regulatory compliance issues and leveraging diversity for new ideas, new products and new revenue streams.

"The best-kept secret of successful leaders is love."

Small wonder then that "the best-kept secret of successful leaders is love," according to researchers James Kouzes and Barry Posner in their seminal book *The Leadership Challenge* based on more than two million interviews and surveys over the last 30 years with leaders all over the world. "Of all the things that sustain a leader over time, love is the most lasting," add Kouzes and Posner. When a leader is in love with the process of leading, he or she has "the fire to ignite other people, see inside other people, to have a greater desire to get things done," noted John H. Stanford, a former Major General in the United States Army, cited in *The Leadership Challenge*. Love in this business context spotlights the humanity of the individual to "experience another human being in his (or her) very uniqueness," according to Viktor Frankl, the psychiatrist and author of *Man's Search for Meaning.* "By his love he (or she) is enabled to see the essential traits and features in the beloved person." Author James Hunter defines love in a business context as "extending yourself to help others" in his book, *World's Most Powerful Leadership Principle.* And one of the 30 definitions of love in the dictionary says love is the "affectionate concern for the well-being of others."

Psychologists tell us that love is a behavior more than simply a feeling, a behavior that champions others, a behavior that validates the dignity and worth of another human being, a behavior that stems from a mindset of caring and sharing, a behavior that compels you to hate the sin but love the sinner. That's why the last sentence in *The Leadership Challenge* by James Kouzes and Barry Posner, summarizes the crux of loving like a leader:

"Leadership is not an affair of the head.
Leadership is an affair of the heart."

As an affair of the heart in helping others grow and develop, love in a business context is what the bible calls "charity" and the Greeks call *agape.* That focus on the soul of a person validates their essence, affirms their sense of purpose and confirms their passionate commitment toward a creative collaborative performance. Then their caring and sharing mindset—their love for each other in a business context—is more meaningful than other forms of love the Greeks identified thousands of years ago. In loving others in a business context, a leader's *agape* reinforces the humanity of others more fully with no self-serving intent. That's why researchers tell us that a loving leader's *agape* is more voluntary than obligatory—beyond the love between obligated family members (*storge*). A loving leader's agape is more supporting and sustaining, according to researchers, than a love rooted in a long lasting marriage (*pragma*); more energizing than flirting *(ludus)* and even more mutually satisfying than sex *(eros)*

"I Love You.
You're Fired!"

Maximizing organizational performance. That's the bottom-line in loving like a leader. It's not about doing something nice or trying to be better liked. As author Ken Blanchard notes in his book, *Helping People Win at Work*:

> *"Servant leadership isn't trying to please everybody or letting the inmates run the prison. It's about unleashing the potential of others."*

Servant leadership is also about "driving the fear out of your organization so that people can perform at their highest level," observes author Gregg Cochlan in his book *Love Leadership*. And love in a business context is not a hugfest Cochlan notes. It's demanding work that challenges a leader's comfort zone and broadens the scope, depth and reach of a leader's emotional intelligence. "It's hard to lead with love," asserts CEO-turned-author Joel Manby in his book *Love Works*. "It's much easier to focus only on hitting the numbers and not worry about the impact our actions have on people." That's why love in a business context requires the self-confidence and poise to step into the shoes of another person; the courage to see the trials and tribulations others see and the fortitude to feel the frustration and concerns of others.

And at times love in the business context can become a tough love where, "leaders discipline people they do like and reward people they don't like," notes former CEO James Autry and Stephen Mitchell in their book *Real Power*. "If you can't say 'I love you, you're fired or 'you're a pain in the ass here's your raise' you shouldn't be in management." That tough love—CARING about the well-being of others based on their behavior not your personal disposition— is the top trait of a leader, according to British historian John Keegan. In his book *The Mask of Command*, Keegan says CARING is more significant of a leadership trait than: knowing what to do, rewarding behavior, taking action or providing example. For those of you who would dismiss this caring aspect of leadership as too "touchy feely" consider that Keegan wrote more than 20 books on the nature of combat and the psychology in battle.

In fact, the significance of affection on the battle field is well documented. A study by sociologists Edward A. Shils and Morris Janowitz concluded a soldier will continue to fight even in a losing battle "as long as he gave affection to and received affection from the other members of his squad. (See General James Mattis, 23). That same kind of affection empowering passionate performance is found in business, according to Dexter Yager, Amway's most successful coach (a.k.a. distributor). He developed more leaders than anyone else in the multi-level marketing industry. Asked his secret to success Yager beamed during a *60 Minutes* nationally televised broadcast:

> *"That's 'cause I love 'em.*
> *That's cause I really love 'em.*
> *They're like my kids."*
> *--Dexter Yager*

Paternalism aside, leaders cultivate a workplace "where people can discover their gifts, share their gifts and most extremely be recognized and appreciated," writes CEO Bob Chapman in his book, *Everybody Matters.* That's why former CEO Gerry Czarnecki says the only way to *"achieve peak performance results consistently over the long run must begin with love. **No leader can be effective without a deep love for people as human beings.**"*

Writing in his book *Lead With Love*, Czarnecki adds: "People will do almost anything if they think they are appreciated and if they are being led by someone who cares. If you can't love quit trying to be a leader." That's why loving leaders do more than engage and energize. They enable and ennoble. They are quick to dignify—not vilify—others. Even if and when they have to fire 'em. With love.

COACHING
Putting Love To Work

As stewards, leaders and their followers are linked to each other in a mindful duet of caring and sharing for one another where one brings out the best in the other. Together the leader and the follower, the coach and the coachee, generate a synergy. That synergy is contagious, especially when a loving coach hears the feint music playing deep inside a coachee. Then the coach—inspired by that music—begins to proverbially tap his or her foot, strum his or her fingers and hum along in rhythm. The coach and the coachee are in tune, fully integrated, completely engaged in a specific task, focused on a specific purpose, and concentrating on a specific outcome. Two minds. Four hands. One vision. They are connected to each other and strengthened by each other the more they come together, one amplifying the sound of the other and both celebrating with a proverbial dance to the ensuing music.

At least that's the insight of executive coach Madeleine Homan-Blanchard: The coach "who is going to make the biggest difference is the one who loves the people being coached." No wonder the "best-kept secret of successful leaders is love," according to James Kouzes and Barry Posner in their book *The Leadership Challenge* based on two million interviews with corporate and non-profit leaders around the world over 25 years. (See introduction, page 9 and Defining Love, page 201.) In coaching others, loving leaders meet face to face. They preface (read pre-face) their relationships with a committed trust and humility where they can be more open with each other, more vulnerable to each other, more accountable by each other, more transparent for each other—and more likely to welcome, savor and digest negative feedback as a professional development opportunity.

That's because loving leaders foster a more intimate communications process with their direct reports. They look into each other's eyes rather than hide behind each other's texting screens. They say what needs to be said in person without feeling virtually oppressed under each other's texting thumbs. And together they celebrate their face-to-face contact, knowing their two-heads-are-better-than-one relationship is distinctly human especially when they realize that human beings are the only animals on earth who mate face to face. They leverage their "mating" relationship to nurture the growth of both the leader and his or her coachee. In nurturing other leaders, each loving leader reaches the pinnacle of leadership (Level 5) in the parlance of author Jim Collins. In his seminal book *Good to Great*, Collins defines a Level 5 leader as one who "blends extreme personal humility with intense professional will."

Feelings Matter Engineers Say

Loving leaders leverage their humility and their intense personal will to achieve outstanding results despite adversity, setbacks, mistakes and failures. And Level 5 leaders lead with the love of a coach who empowers with something more than their technical skills. Just ask technically proficient engineering and math whiz leaders at Google. Their technical skills figured dead last in an extensive company-wide employee survey to determine key behaviors of the most effective leaders. The first three traits according to the survey focused on managers (a.k.a loving leaders) who have a FEELING for leading, who care for and share with others: They are good coaches. They empower their teams. And they express interest in their team members' success and well-being.

The next four traits focused on communication and career development: They are results oriented and predictable in their expectations and support over the long term. They are good communicators who listen. They help employees with career development. And loving leaders have a clear vision and strategy for their team. Feelings matter in effective leadership observed Adam Bryant, the leadership columnist for *The New York Times*. He summarized the Google study on effective managers with this insight: "What employees valued most were even-keeled bosses who made time for one-on-one meetings, who helped people puzzle through problems by asking questions, not dictating answers, and who took an interest in employees' lives and careers." Feelings count. That's why author Tom Peters says, "leadership is 100 percent about emotion." Without feeling, Aristotle noted there can be no leadership: "One who attempts to move people to thought or action must concern themselves with their emotions," Aristotle observed. "If he (or she) touches only their minds, he (or she) is unlikely to move them to action or to a change of mind, the motivations of which lie deep in the realm of passions."

That's why a leader's empathetic mindset drives their ethical behavior, one becomes an expression of the other. A leader's outside behavior becomes the inside feeling and the inside feeling becomes the outside behavior, like the seamless sides of a Mobius Strip, notes Harvard's Erica Ariel Fox in her book *Winning from Within*. No wonder today's most successful leaders (a.k.a. loving leaders) see themselves not as a Leader of the Pack fueled with pride and pretense, bombast and bravura that ebbs and flows. Instead, today's most successful leaders see themselves as a Leader with a Pact fueled with humility, integrity and love that ebbs and grows.

Unpacking Your
Personal Baggage

In developing that pact with their followers, loving leaders first unpack their personal baggage. They realize that becoming a leader first means you have to put down your personal baggage before you can lift others up. In sorting through their personal baggage, leaders have to first examine who they are and what they believe before they can make love like a leader. They seek first to understand and accept who they are with a greater sense of authenticity, transparency and vulnerability.

That's why they begin their quest to become a loving leader by embarking on "a great journey into your own soul" as Jeff Immelt, the CEO at General Electric defines the initial step in becoming a leader. However, in setting out on that journey into your own soul, emerging loving leaders have to beware of tripping over their own egos when they need too much and heed too little. And most significantly, nascent loving leaders have to beware and be wary of the following Needs that can jeopardize their ability to love and undermine their capacity to lead. Leo Buscaglia lists these Nine Needs in his book *Loving Each Other*:

- The Need to be always right.
- The Need to be first in everything.
- The Need to be consistently in control.
- The Need to be perfect.
- The Need to be loved by everyone.
- The Need to possess.
- The Need to blame.
- The Need to dominate.
- The Need to manipulate.

In addition to containing and controlling those self-serving needs, the most effective leaders heed the needs of others. They nurture others. In nurturing, in connecting with others, the most effective leaders rely less on texting and e-mails and more on face-to-face listening, affirming and communicating. In nurturing others, a leader invariably unearths hidden resources, leverages differences, fosters greater productivity and mines increased profitability that makes every day pay day. However in nurturing others, leaders know only too well that their date book is as important as their checkbook; their time as valued as their money. As poet Kahlil Gibran said: "You give but little when you give of your possessions. It is when you give of yourself that you truly give." In giving of yourself, a loving leader thrives on people and potential more than on power and position.

Those who love to lead ad hoc thrive on power and position. Those who lead to love 24/7 thrive on people and potential. In loving, the most effective leaders take on "life's greatest challenge," asserts author Leo Buscaglia in his book *LOVE*. He writes that love: "Requires more subtlety, flexibility, sensitivity, understanding, acceptance, tolerance, knowledge and strength than any other human emotion."

Yet the results can be outstanding as author Ken Blanchard notes in his book *Lead With LUV* with co-author Colleen Barrett. "Leading with love is the only way to get great results and human satisfaction at the same time." No wonder that Margie Blanchard, the co-founder of the Ken Blanchard Companies, flatly declares that leadership is love. "Leadership is not about love. It is love. It's loving your mission, loving your customers and loving yourself enough to get out of the way so that other people can be magnificent."

How Many Souls On Board?

What if you thought of your organization as if it were a 747 jet flying at 35,000 feet with so many souls on board? Not passengers. Not employees. Souls. Think of the implications of that provocative question: How many souls on board? That's the question that Air Traffic Controllers pose to pilots during an emergency. The word "souls" more clearly communicates the inclusive list of humans at risk (passengers, pilots and crew) and acknowledges to the pilot that the controller realizes the seriousness of the emergency and that he or she is personally committed to leading all souls to a safe landing. The implication: we are all in this together. We need each other. We have to work with each other—and for each other—to achieve our common destiny: a safe landing.

That realization that we are all in this together no matter where you are sitting in this organization—in First Class or Coach, in the Pilot's seat or in Aft seat—stems from a feeling of caring and sharing with others, a feeling of interdependence on each other, a sense of love of and for each other that feeds the organization in general and the leaders in particular to better adapt to changing conditions in real time.

With a focus on their collective souls, loving leaders tap into an ever-widening and enriching treasure chest of humanity with all of its attendant inspiration, imagination and innovation. Their caring for and sharing with others foments a spirit stronger than teamwork, a synergistic spirit that bolsters the bottom line with love. After all people are "desperately motivated to love something well and be loved," observed David Brooks, in his column in *The New York Times*. He said a "core task of communities" is "to widen and deepen opportunities for love."

Love spawns caring and sharing leaders who focus that feeling into a purpose that attracts others. Maybe that's why Woodrow Wilson, the former president of the United States, said that you can't lead unless you act "under the impulse of a profound sympathy with those whom he leads." The dictionary defines sympathy as "understanding between people, a common feeling" that reaches deep into all souls on board.

"The warm fuzzy stuff is hard."

G uy Kawasaki, the founder of AllTop, the on-line magazine rack of the web and the chief executive officer of Garage Technical Ventures, a capital investment firm for early-stage startups, remembers the first time he earned a management position: "I found out how hard it is to lead and manage people," Kawasaki noted in Adam Bryant's book *The Corner Office*. "The warm fuzzy stuff is hard. The quantitative stuff is easy. You either don't do much of that as a manager or you have people working for you do it." But of course leaders can't delegate the "warm fuzzy stuff."

AFTERWORD

QUICK & EASY WAYS

To Do

The Warm Fuzzy Stuff

Looking for a quick and easy way to sharpen your skills as a loving leader? Say "Thank you" a lot more and consider a stint as a United Way loaned executive and maybe even enjoy an evening at the opera. And here you will learn the secret to dealing with people you don't like but first turn the page to remind yourself why anyone would ever follow you if you didn't have positional authority.

Why Would Anyone Follow You?

O f course your employees will follow your lead if your name is inscribed on door to your company, printed on the front part of their paychecks or listed near the top of an organizational chart. At least for a while. However the most effective leaders know their followers will follow them even farther down the road to success the more the leader lives up to his or her role as their loving leader. With a sharing and caring mindset, loving leaders contribute to the growth of the bottom-line by keeping their followers top of mind. They are as concerned about the needs and interests of their employees as they are about the needs and interests of the company or organization.

That's why loving leaders—especially those who reside deep in the bowels of an organization below the deepest organization chart without any formal leadership title, position or budget—more readily attract and retain followers. They express compassion FOR others without trying to impress their passions on others. Their compassion for others gains and retains followers based on a mutual trust that is given not earned, a trust that is expected not inspected and a trust that is amplified not verified. They acknowledge that well-worn bromide that no one cares how much you know until they know how much you care. And they know you're a loving leader not because of your place at the top of the organization chart but by your place in the hearts and minds of your followers. They follow you because: "You build trust. You foster collaboration. You model the way, set a good example, challenge the process, are clear about your values, your vision for the future, and your ability to enlist others in your vision," notes James Kouzes, leadership development researcher and co-author of *The Leadership Challenge*. "You make other people feel strong and capable. You search for opportunities to grow, innovate and improve."[*]

*Source: James Kouzes, Voice America Business Channel radio interview with Kate Ebner, the host of *Visionary Leader, Extraordinary Life.*

Loving Leaders
Say Thank You

You're a proficient leader. Your bottom-line is strong. Your results consistently improving. And now after reading **LOVING Like a Leader**, you have reaffirmed what you always knew: Caring for others makes good business sense. But still this idea of love in the workplace makes you uncomfortable. You are not the out-going, buddy-buddy type. Nor do you want to be. You are good at what you do. And yes you'd like to be even better. You'd like to leverage this idea of love in the workplace—but on your terms. You can. Start by simply saying "Thank you" even more often. Thank your staff collectively and individually. With even more sincerity. With even more enthusiasm. With even more specificity. And with an even broader and brighter appreciative smile. Then you will nourish more of that expected behavior and performance enhancements while also nurturing a caring and a loving working environment.

As former CEO and author Max De Pree observes: "The first responsibility of a leader is to define reality. The last is to say 'thank you.'" However saying thank you isn't as easy as it sounds. Particularly for men. And that's not as sexist as it sounds. It's an observation based on experience. Just ask the 17 men who took part in an impromptu study that leadership development expert and famed author Tom Peters conducted. The study, albeit highly unscientific and statistically flawed, is still a wake-up call to male leaders in particular. In a three-week span, Peters flew 21 times. On each flight he had only one seatmate. They totaled 17 men and four women. Peters counted the number of times his seatmate said "thank you" to the flight attendant for routine transactions: a refill on their drink, a hot towel, or a served dinner etc.

The results: the four women seatmates said "thank you" 23 times. The 17 men, numbering more than four times the women, said "thank you" fewer than half as many times (11). Saying "thank you" is the first step in appreciating others, in recognizing their performance and adding meaning to their work. Feelings matter in sustaining results. "The way your people feel about you, the company, your products and services and themselves when they are at work is the critical element in their performance, productivity and output," observe Brian Tracey and Dr. Peter Chee in their book, *12 Disciplines of Leadership Excellence.* "The more time you take to tell and show your people that they are valuable and important, and that you care about them, the better manager you will be and the better results you will get." As author Mark Crowley notes in his book *Lead from the Heart:* "Employees want to feel that their work matters, that they are appreciated by their boss and respected in their organization, and that they are given an opportunity to contribute something meaningful."

Leveraging Your
OPERA-ting Capital

How do loving leaders hone their feeling for leading from the heart? Put yourself in the shoes of the newly appointed division president who visited his boss for their first one-on-one meeting. He had a file of pending issues to discuss but the chairman of this billion-dollar company this morning seemed more interested in talking more about the opera than his company's OPERAtions. Whoa there! What does an appreciation of the opera have to do with leading a multi-billion dollar global company? Nothing. Or everything. As Fred Plitkin writes in his book *Opera 101:* "Opera-going at its best is about the rekindling of the soul, about having an open window into what makes us human."

Husbanding that humanity —or at least harboring that humanity with a greater sense of feeling — is a key leadership skill, especially relevant when the Chairman noted in passing that the word <u>opera</u> in Italian means <u>work</u>. Consider how famous movies use the music of the opera to add passion and power to emotion-packed portrayals of the human condition such as ***Fatal Attraction*** (*Madame Butterfly* by Giacomo Puccini), ***The Godfather*** (*La Travisata* by Giuseppe Verdi) and ***Shawshank Redemption*** (*The Marriage of Figaro by Amadeus Mozart).* Vicariously walking on that tension wire of life magnified in the movies and portrayed so personally on the live opera stage, leaders in the audience are imbued with an exaggerated sense of human behavior. They face tragic consequences on the opera stage that break a leader out of his or her personal bubble and more fully inform their heightened sense of humanity in general and their specific ability to lead with feeling in particular. As former CEO David D'Alessandro writes in his book *Executive Warfare*, your perspective in life away from the job is critical in establishing your leadership skills: "You cannot develop perspective if your entire life revolves around your job. To get to the top—and stay there—you need to be able to lead human beings. And, the only way to learn how to lead is to live." Living life writ large is the hallmark of the opera with its over-the-top staging and its heart-wrenching arias of raw emotion that grip your throat and gnaw deep into your skin with an escalating passion; an agonizing loss, or an ever-hopeful day of reckoning and reward.

In Giochino Rossini's opera *The Barber of Seville*, Figaro sings about how happy he is to serve his customers "quick as lighting." He sings how much he enjoys being in demand by his customers. They call out his name: Figaro, Figaro, Figaro. And how proud he is, having earned a reputation not only as a barber "of quality" but also as a man of so many talents that he is also known as his city's handyman. The pride of workmanship beams in the voice of Figaro. Likewise the showcasing of a full range of human emotions in any opera and our vicarious experience of love and anguish, joy and sorrow from an audience's perspective rejuvenates our own ability to love. And lead.

Appreciating Others

"Employees want to feel that their work matters, that they are appreciated by their boss and respected in their organization, and that they are given an opportunity to contribute something meaningful."

Mark Crowley
Lead from the Heart:

Dealing With People You Don't Like

How do you deal with people you have to work with — colleagues, bosses, direct reports etc.— if you don't even like them? Love 'em. Behave like a loving leader: treat others with dignity and respect. Listen intently. Focus on solutions not blame. Celebrate diversity. Leverage differences. Fake it at first but then you will come to love the people you don't like. That's the insight of C.S. Lewis. The philosopher and author says: "Do not waste time bothering me whether you 'love' your neighbor, act as if you did. As soon as we do this we find one of the great secrets when you are behaving as if you loved someone, you will presently come to love them."

Focus on the "behaviors of love" (a.k.a. leadership) not your feelings of disdain for others, notes James Hunter in his book *The World's Most Powerful Leadership Principle: How to Become a Servant Leader.* Don't complain. Just do it and soon you'll start loving people you don't even like. During a Q&A session Hunter conducted, one participant beamed at his new-found understanding of this fake-it-until-you-make-it initiative: "Oh I get it: You're trying to get us all to start liking each other more aren't you?

"No that's not it," Hunter quickly replied. "I am not trying to get you to like each other. I am trying to get you to love each other. I am not concerned with how you feel about each other, but I am concerned with how you BEHAVE toward each other. Forget about your feelings. For now. Focus on how we are treating each other. You'll find that the feelings will follow later."

Loving leaders understand that you treat others the way you want to be treated and they will begin treating you the same way. With love.

On-the-Job Training
For Loving Leaders

You don't need to be an opera aficionado to vicariously experience a more poignant perspective on the human condition that sharpens your emotional intelligence and extends your ability to feel what others are feeling as a loving leader. Working fulltime as a fundraiser for the United Way for three months while my employer continued to pay my salary, I saw how vulnerable all of us really are to changing conditions (illness, injury, aging or loss of a spouse or a job etc.) regardless of their zip code or bank account. And for the first time in my life, I understood with a deeper insight the wisdom of Chief Seattle when he said:

> *Each of us is but one thread within the web of life. Whatever we do to the web we do to ourselves. All things are bound together. All things connect.*
>
> *-Chief Seattle*

My role as an United Way loaned executive helped me more accurately find and define threads in me that I didn't even know existed, threads that helped me sew my sense of my own humanity more fully into the fabric of my life, my family and friends, my company, my community, and ultimately into my thinking about love and leadership that resulted in this book. And in the process, I discovered dangling threads in others that helped me weave a more diverse, more open, more responsive and more understanding mindset of a loving leader. Learning to love others in a business context on the job, I enriched my sense of empathy for people like Linda, homeless for six months. Linda winced at the memory of the pain that ripped through her body as she walked the city streets in the raw six-degree cold in the dead of winter in the middle of the night. And now thanks to the United Way, Linda had a loving and supporting environment to find her own thread, an artistic thread that she wove that night in front of me and 15 Target store employees on the United Way campaign trail. Her art celebrated the bull and the eagle of her Native American heritage. Her poetry saluted the strength that *Mother Earth* gave her "to walk in Beauty, to be wise of everything around me."

Meanwhile I can still hear the anguish in the voice of the manager of a Best Buy telling his employees when he was a boy that a tornado blew his house away. He still remembers how the American Red Cross and the United Way stepped in to give that scared eight-year-old some sense of security and stability. Indeed, we are all vulnerable to the tornadoes of life. You learn just how vulnerable when you accompany a United Way volunteer who regularly delivers meals to the elderly and others who are virtually prisoners in their own homes.

Lifting Others Up
Without Stepping On Their Toes

Rosa opened the door and smiled when she recognized the regular Meals on Wheels driver. She motioned to me to put her lunch on the table and proudly introduced me to her four grandchildren. Their pictures in a photo cube served as the table's centerpiece. Rosa explained that she could no longer cook for herself because she doesn't drive and can't get to the grocery store very often now that her husband had recently died. Her grandchildren live in another state and she's planning on moving there soon but right now she is trying to fend for herself as best as she can with help from the United Way in her time of need. "They care," Rosa said of the United Way in her thick Italian accent. "They are there to lift me up, just like that." Rosa smiled again and pointed to a poem she had framed and hung in her hallway.

The poem titled *Footprints In The Sand* by Margaret Fishback expresses the poet's feeling of abandonment when the second set of footprints walking with her suddenly disappears in her moment of need. But the poem says that a voice whispered to her that when she saw only one set of footprints "it was then that I carried you." Rosa's admiration of that image —of one-set of footprints in the sand—helped me better learn and better understand the art of loving like a leader: Lifting others up without stepping on their toes.

APPENDIX

How to Hone
Your Sense of Humor

Here are specific strategies you can use to become an even more committed loving leader. Laugh a lot. See Laughing like a leader (page 220) and a special 10-page section on honing your sense of humor (221-230). After all, the essence of humor is love according to philosopher and historian Thomas Carlyle.

LAUGHING
Like a Loving Leader

H ow do you build trust as a loving leader? Laugh a lot. Poet Maya Angelou observed that she couldn't trust anyone who didn't laugh. Laughter is vital to clear thinking and less stress according to medical researchers. Laughter increases your brain's oxygen supply and makes you feel so energized that hundreds of people gather in public parks every day in 72 countries to laugh out loud as a breathing exercise. They are members of the 16,000 yoga laughter clubs that have formed since 1995. "Laughter expels more of the bad "air" in our minds and bodies and makes room for 25% more oxygen to think more quickly and act more precisely," says Dr. Madan Kataria, who founded laughter yoga movement in Mumbai, India.

No wonder that loving leaders laugh a lot. And why not as comedian Victor Borge noted: "Laugher is the shortest distance between two people." Loving leaders embrace the notion that humor is a "vital tool of leadership," as Dr. Gerald D. Bell states. At least that's what the data showed when Dr. Bell's researchers surveyed 2,700 employees over two years on what traits contributed most to an effective leader. Having a good sense of humor and a strong work ethic were mentioned twice as often as any other trait of the most effective leaders.

That's why loving leaders hone their sense of humor. They realize that a keen sense of humor broadens their perspective as Rev. Billy Graham said and helps us "to overlook the unbecoming, understand the unconventional, tolerate the unpleasant, overcome the unexpected and outlast the unbearable." That's why more than 9 out of 10 executives in a Robert Half International survey believe a sense of humor is important for career advancement, coping with stress and guarding against a cynical or sarcastic defensive tone that spawns greater conflict. And the essence of humor? It's love according to philosopher and historian Thomas Carlyle. That's why loving leaders log plenty of "smileage," laughing all the way to the bank and beyond.

SEASONING
Your Sense of Humor

SEASON is an acrostic for 6 ways that you can use humor to engage others, ease tension, enhance more effective teamwork and sustain a loving culture filled with heart-felt dignity and respect. The 6 ways to enhance your humor are: ***Substituting, Exaggerating, Associating, Skewing, Opposing and Narrowing.***

S - Substituting

When you substitute, you bait and switch.

You bait your audience with a straight line (the setup) then you substitute an unexpected but <u>related</u> concept (the punchline).

- Citing the wedding night of 86-year-old Hugh Hefner to a 26-year-old, Jay Leno substituted: "She wore Channel No. 5. He wore Febreze."

- Commenting on the nomination of John Kerry as Secretary of State, Jay Leno substituted that John Kerry's face "is longer than mine. He looks more like Secretariat of State."

E - Exaggerating

When you exaggerate, you stretch a point of view.

- Observing the longevity of Regis Philbin still hosting a TV talk show at 80, David Letterman exaggerated: "I don't want to say that Regis is old but his first co-host was Eve."

- Reacting to wintry weather in New York City, David Letterman exaggerated: "It was so cold today driving to work (in New York City), the navigation lady in my car directed me to Saudi Arabia.

- Noting the low water pressure in his apartment, comedian Rodney Dangerfield exaggerated: "The plumbing in my apartment is so bad that if I want to take a bath on Sunday I have to start running the water on Wednesday."

A - Associating

*When you associate,
you link two <u>unrelated</u> ideas.*

- Associating his roommate's initials with an expletive, Oscar Madison in the movie The *Odd Couple* says to Felix Unger, "You write me these notes and sign them FU. It took me three months to realize FU stood for Felix Unger.

- Associating her repeated appearances in court with playing tennis too much, David Letterman says that Lindsay Lohan had taken the oath in court so often the Hollywood actress had suffered "bible elbow."

- Associating a baby's high chair to a garbage truck, Jay Leno says: "Babies are so overweight they now have high chairs that beep when you move them backwards."

- Associating, Donald Trump's trademark bright flowing hair to cotton candy, Seth MacFarlane says Trump "must have fallen head first into a cotton candy machine."

S – Skewing

When you skew, you twist the intended meaning.

Yogi Berra, the New York Yankee Hall of Fame baseball star of yesteryear, became as famous off the field for inadvertently skewing the English language in ways that triggered perplexed smiles if not head-scratching bewilderment. And people laughed at his screw ups or more to the point his *"skew-ups."*

- Noting how popular a restaurant had become, Yogi Berra skewed: "That restaurant is always so crowded, nobody goes there anymore."

- Noting that Mickey Mantle could bat both right and left-handed (ambidextrous), Yogi Berra skewed that his Yankee teammate was "amphibious."

- Introduced to a pretty woman who remarked how cool he looked in his light summer suit, Yogi Berra skewed: "Thanks, you don't look so hot yourself."

O - Opposing

When you oppose,
you redirect the expected order.

- Rodney Dangerfield redirected the expected order and reinforced his signature statement ("I get no respect") with this opposing observation: "When I was a boy I was so poor, I got batteries. Toys not included."

- W.C. Fields redirected the expected order with this opposing observation: "I am free of all prejudice. I hate everyone equally."

- Golda Meir redirected the expected order with this opposing observation: "Don't be humble. You're not that great."

- And the apocryphal story of the Soviet Union issuing a new postage stamp redirected the expected order with this opposing observation: "The new postage stamp with Joseph Stalin's picture on didn't stick so well. Seems the Russians were spitting on the wrong side."

Beware of Sarcasm

In using humor, the most effective leaders, guard against sarcasm's harsh cousin—sardonic humor— that is mockingly derisive. Beware what works for Lisa Lampanelli—the *Queen of Mean*—on stage in a comedy roast never works in a staff meeting no matter how tongue-in-cheek the presentation. After all, the word "sarcasm" stems from the Greek word "to tear flesh." Self-deprecating sarcasm is most effective where what you say is directly opposed—the opposite—of what the listener expects, such as: "Oh that was a smart move," you hear yourself saying when you drop a pile of papers.

N - NARROWING

When you narrow,
you limit the intended meaning.

- Albert Einstein, the founder of the theory of relativity, was taking a tour of Warner Brother's studio when Jack Warner stopped Einstein and narrowed his sites, saying: "I too have a theory on relatives. Don't hire them."

- A teacher asked a first grader why he was exposing his stomach. The boy complained his stomach hurt. Then he promptly narrowed his sites saying the principal told him to "stick it out" until noon. Then if his stomach was still hurting he could go home.

- A 5-year-old boy crashed his dad's car into the garage. The boy then narrowed his sites, noting that he put the car's transmission into "R" for race.

- A 3-year-old making toast narrowed her sites, saying said she "flushed" her bread in the toaster.

Getting Started
Sharpening Your Sense of Humor
next page.

Sharpening
Your Sense of Humor

Sharpen your sense of humor using these 6 ways to SEASON your prepared remarks. It's easy to get started switching, stretching, linking, twisting, redirecting and limiting your words, thoughts and ideas to SEASON your sense of humor.SEASON is an acrostic to unleash your sense of humor through:

Substituting

Exaggerating

Associating

Skewing

Opposing

Narrowing

Let's begin by:

SUBSTITUTING with your own version of *SWITCHING* when someone asks what's for dinner *(reservations)* or when someone wants to hear your own version of the five food groups (*Salty, Sugary, Gooey Crunchy and Sticky*).

EXAGGERATING with your own version of STRETCHING a point the way Mark Russell does in explaining the concept of a trillion dollars: "A trillion is a number so high that if you stood on the payment book you'd experience weightlessness."

ASSOCIATING with your own version of LINKING two unrelated things. As the wit said: "Statistics are like bikinis. It is not what they reveal that counts. But what they conceal."

SKEWING with your own version of *TWISTING* the intended meaning. Consider how the native of Liverpool, England visiting the United States for the first time responded when asked *"How do you find the United States? John Lennon, the extraordinary musician, singer and songwriter of Beatle fame, retorted: "Take a left at Greenland."*

OPPOSING with your own version of REDIRECTING the expected order such as Mark

Twain's apology to his wife for not wearing a tie to visit an influential neighbor. Twain returned home, found a tie and had it delivered to the neighbor later that day. The enclosed note read: *"A little while ago I visited you without my tie for about a half hour. The missing tie is enclosed. Kindly gaze at it for 30 minutes then return it to me."*

NARROWING with your own version of *LIMITING* the intended meaning such as the sign in a hospital laboratory: *"Be nice to bacteria. It is the only culture some people have."*

SEASON-ed Stories

To stimulate your sense of humor, here are stories that illustrate how you might use four of the six SEASONings.

OPPOSING

Consider this example of OPPOSING—redirecting the expected order —to spark your sense of humor.

The dichotomy was strident: a pristine well-polished, manicured politician vs. a grimy, scrappy dirty-finger nailed coal miner. And the leader is? Yep you guessed it—the coal miner. Even John F. Kennedy—the well-manicured politician—learned something about emotional intelligence in particular and personal leadership in general from that coal miner, a lesson that all leaders need to heed: *Don't judge a book by its cover.* It happened during the 1960 presidential campaign. Kennedy met the coal miner one day during a campaign stop in West Virginia.

Kennedy wore his $1,000 suit and a $100 haircut. The coal miner wore ragged overalls and coal dust smudges on his face that could not cover the wrinkles of working in the mines all his life. The coal miner looked up at Kennedy and scornfully said: "Senator, they say you were born with a silver spoon in your mouth, and that you've never had to really put in a day's work. Is that right?" Kennedy stammered and pawed at the ground with his $500 shoes while the national media cameras hovered over him like hungry tigers.

Finally Kennedy, virtually choking on his proverbial silver spoon, looked down at the old snaggle-toothed, leather-faced, coal miner and finally admitted: "Well, I guess that's about right. I haven't worked as hard as you have." Kennedy braced himself for the expected backlash. But then the coal miner looked up at Kennedy and said: "Well don't worry Senator. You haven't missed a darn thing." Kennedy laughed. The salivating media sighed. And the miner grinned, satisfied if not comfortable with his lot in life and knowing that he had just taught the future President of the United States a key lesson: don't assume the facts in any situation. Practice CYA: Check your assumptions.

ASSOCIATING

*Consider this example of
ASSOCIATING—linking the concept
to something unrelated—to trigger
your sense of humor and a laugh or
two.*

The new housekeeper working for a priest needed to alert her boss that something was wrong. "Father, your TV is broken," the housekeeper said to the Priest. The Priest corrected his housekeeper: "That's our TV, not mine. It is the entire Church's TV. I have taken an oath of poverty. I can't own anything." The new housekeeper understood but must have forgotten because a few weeks later she announced to the Priest: "Your DVR is not working." Once again the Priest explained his vow of poverty and how the DVR is "ours" not his and that the whole congregation in fact actually owns the DVR, the TV and everything else in his home.

A month later the Priest is hosting a meeting with his boss, the Bishop. The Housekeeper interrupts their meeting. There's an emergency in the house. This time the Housekeeper knows the drill: "Father, there's a mouse under OUR bed." The bishop's eyes nearly popped out of his head. The Priest choked in embarrassment. The housekeeper blushed.

NARROWING

Consider this example of NARROWING —limiting the meaning of your focus— to trigger a laugh.

Three men arrive at a train station 30-minutes before the train is ready for boarding. They decided to get a sandwich in a diner next to the train station. They were having such a good time that they forgot about the train. And suddenly they heard the train's whistle. Their train was already beginning to leave the station. All three of them run to catch the train. Two of them got on board. The third started to cry: "I missed my train." And then the same person turned his crying into laughter. A bystander said to him: "Let me get you some help. You are very emotional right now. You missed your train and you are crying and then laughing about it. I really better get you some help." But then the would-be passenger says, "No you don't understand. You know those two other guys? Well, they came to the train station to SEE ME OFF."

SKEWING

Consider this example of SKEWING—twisting the intended meaning—to tickle your funny bone.

The 13-year-old was concerned. Her parents were refinancing their house again. Their daughter needed clarification: "But dad haven't you been paying on the house all these years," Amy wondered? Yes her dad assured her. Amy looked around her bedroom like a queen looks at her throne and said with a good deal of exasperation: "Well, is MY ROOM at least paid for?"

ADDENDUM

Leadership Mints
At Your Fingertips

Here's a menu that will help you quickly scan the 77 Leadership Mints at-a-glance. See the Behavioral Index (page 232) for a list of the Mints organized according to 18 leadership behaviors from adapting and affirming to caring and commitment to trust and vulnerability.

To help you better apply all 77 Leadership Mints, see the Overview (page 234) that provides a quick summary on each of the 77 Leadership Mints.

See pages 237-240 for a listing of all 77 EngageMINTS, the key one-line statement that captures the crux of the learning in each Mint.

To view the chronological contents of the book see page 241. And to get a list of all 77-plus leadership books quoted in this book see page 260.

Behavioral Index

Here are the 18 different leadership behaviors organized alphabetically & listed by Mint Number in this book.

ADAPTING	**Mint 20**..... To the feelings of others **Mint 33**..... To the interests of others **Mint 40**..... To the perspectives of others **Mint 47**..... To the needs of others **Mint 53**......To office visitors **Mint 73**..... To change
AFFIRMING	**Mint 18**..... Make others feel important **Mint 21**..... Share in another's happiness **Mint 22**..... Acknowledge another's reality **Mint 30**..... Validate others **Mint 63**..... Honor others
ALIGNING	**Mint 23**.....Getting to know others **Mint 24**.....Pollinating others **Mint 32**.....Getting to know yourself **Mint 56** ... Creatively connecting with others **Mint 57**.....Standing up for your beliefs **Mint 58**.....Working on purpose **Mint 62**......Pulling your own strings
AUTHENTICITY	**Mint 8**.......Be comfortable in your own skin **Mint 9**...... Be transparent **Mint 46**.....Stay focused on who you are **Mint 66**.... Express your integrity
CARING	**Mint 1**..... Sparking the hidden value in others **Mint 3**..... Crying for others **Mint 5**..... Bringing out the best in others **Mint 13**... Supporting others **Mint 14**....Comforting others **Mint 42**....Pre-serving others
COMMITMENT	**Mint 17**.....Rewarding loyalty **Mint 36**.... Beyond appointments **Mint 55**.....Investing completely in each other **Mint 59**.....Persisting to help others **Mint 60**.....Professionalism 24/7
EMOTIONAL INTELLIGENCE	**Mint 7**...... Stepping outside of yourself **Mint 11**.....Beware of your pedigree **Mint 25**.....Sensitivity to community **Mint 45**.....Reining in your ego **Mint 50** ....Patience before taking action **Mint 52**.....Hiding behind technology **Mint 54**.....Sensitivity to others

EMPATHY	**Mint 4**...... Listening intently and exclusively **Mint 35**.... Persuading others **Mint 39**.... Criticizing others
EXPECTATIONS	**Mint 28**.... Breathing life into others **Mint 29**.... Searching for the beauty within **Mint 34**... Show by example.
HUMILITY	**Mint 37**.....Dare to be humble **Mint 44**.....Swallow your feedback **Mint 61**.....Striving to be the best not the biggest
INSPIRATION	**Mint 12**......Building confidence in others **Mint 51**..... WOW 'em with feeling **Mint 75**......Keep hope alive **Mint 76**.......Marching on regardless of age
PERSISTENCE	**Mint 69**..... Rejecting rejection **Mint 70**..... Friction makes others shine **Mint 71**..... Winning despite the odds **Mint 72**..... Succeeding after a tough start
PERSPECTIVE	**Mint 41**... Seeing another's point of view **Mint 48**.... Parlay your patience. **Mint 49**.... Slow down **Mint 67**... Learning from failure **Mint 68**... Cashing in on mistakes **Mint 74**... Preempting the pity party
RESPECT	**Mint 15**.... . For retirees **Mint 16**.... For teenagers **Mint 31**... For the incarcerated **Mint 38**... For all regardless of status
SYNERGY	**Mint 6**... Interdependence **Mint 65** ... Fierce Conversations **Mint 77**..... Leveraging your competition
TRUST	**Mint 26**.... Founded on relationships **Mint 27**.... Trust given not earned
VULNERABILITY	**Mint 2** ..... Suffering for others **Mint 10**.... Becoming more credible **Mint 43**.... Conquering your weakness
WRITING	**Mint 19**..... Saying you're sorry **Mint 64**.... Setting expectations

OVERVIEW
77 Leadership Mints

Part I: COMPASSION

Compassion takes courage. It takes courage to lead others with love, to bare your feelings *(Mint 2)*, to listen completely (Mint 4) and to step out from behind your position or title *(Mint 7)* and assume long-term responsibility for your employees *(Mint 13)*. Declaring your interdependence on others *(Mint 6)*, you bring out the best in others *(Mint 5)* and spark the hidden value in others *(Mint 1)*. You become more authentic *(Mint 8)*, more transparent *(Mint 9)*, more willing to own your mistakes *(Mint 10)* and more apt to apologize *(Mint 19)*.

With compassion, you more readily cry tears of joy or tears of sorrow for others *(Mint 3)*.

With compassion, you fortify the self-esteem of struggling employees *(Mint 12)* so they can be even more productive *(Mint 14)*.

With compassion, you demonstrate respect for retirees *(Mint 15)* and for those who don't agree with you *(Mint 16)*.

With compassion, you learn to treat others first class for their loyalty and commitment not because of their economic status *(Mint 17)*.

With compassion, you make others feel comfortable around you *(Mint 20)*. You make others feel important *(Mint 18)*. And you become more self-aware of your inherent blind spots *(Mint 11)*.

With compassion, you more readily acknowledge the cultural and social gaps in your heritage and avow to bridge the gaps with understanding and empathy *(Mint 13)*.

Part II: CONNECTION

In connecting with others, leaders invest their time and effort. They get to know others more personally *(Mint 23)*, affirm their reality *(Mint 22)*, trigger their sense of well-being *(Mint 21)*, inspire their talents *(Mint 24)* and reward (Mint 54). They lead by example (Mint 34), invest in trusting relationships *(Mint 25)*, develop on-going trust *(Mint 26)*, treat others the way they prefer (Mint 33) and WOW others with feeling (Mint 51).

In connecting with others, leaders discern the hidden dignity and worth of others *(Mints 28)*, enhance their self-esteem *(Mint 29)*, leverage their expectations of others *(Mint 27)*, and build synergy with a sense of interdependence (Mint 6). Leaders also make the familiar more interesting (Mint 41) and give others the VIP treatment *(Mint 30)*.

In connecting with others, leaders also learn to discipline themselves *(Mint 32) to* keep commitments *(Mint 36)* to maintain the self-esteem of others *(Mint 44)*, to exercise patience *(Mint 48)* to slow things down *(Mint 49)* and to negotiate a more comprehensive result *(Mint 50)* that adds value to others *(Mint 56)*.

In connecting to others, leaders also make a 100% commitment to their long-term partnerships *(Mint 55)*, establish a comfort level with others *(Mint 53)*, dare to be humble (Mint 37) and ironically gain strength from their vulnerability (Mint 43). In addition, leaders also hone their sense of perspective *(Mint 40)*, wear appropriate masks *(Mint 47)* and refuse to hide behind their technology *(Mint 52)*. Leaders are clear about who they really are (Mint 46), guard against an erupting ego *(Mint 45)* and find ways to argue without being argumentative *(Mint 35)*.

Part III: CONVICTION

With conviction that stimulates love, the leader develops values (*Mint 57*), purpose *(Mint 58)*, long-term commitment *(Mint 59)* and meaningful one-on-one meetings *(Mint 65)*.

With conviction that stimulates love, leaders develop their integrity *(Mint 33)*, overcome adversity *(Mint 70)*, beat the odds *(Mint 71)* and rebound from a tough start *(Mint 72)*.

With conviction that stimulates love, leaders persist 24/7 *(Mint 60)* toward continuous improvement (Mint 61) with integrity (Mint 66) and a steady hand (Mint 62) toward something bigger than themselves *(Mint 63)* that engages their direct reports personally with their interests (Mint 64).

With conviction that stimulates love, leaders more readily leverage change *(Mint 73)*, thrive on competition (*Mint 77*) and fight off the ravages of time (*Mint 76*).

With conviction that stimulates love, leaders maintain a positive attitude (*Mint 74*), keep hope alive *(Mint 75)*, learn from failure *(Mint 67)*, reject rejection *(Mint 69)* and innovate from their mistakes *(Mint 68)*.

EngageMINTS

A one-line
key learning summary of
a Leadership Mint story.

Part I
COMPASSION

Mint 1   Unlock the treasure buried in your employees.
Mint 2   Beware of walling yourself off from others.
Mint 3   Shed your tears for others not for yourself.
Mint 4   Appreciate others with intentional listening.
Mint 5   Love others to bring out the best in them.

Mint 6   Relying on others fortifies your leadership.
Mint 7   Step outside of yourself to gain insight into others.
Mint 8   Be comfortable in your own skin.
Mint 9   Be real to close the deal.
Mint 10   Vulnerability can be a source of strength.

Mint 11   Remember where you came from.
Mint 12   Preserve the self-confidence of others.
Mint 13   Shining the light on others reflects well on you.
Mint 14   Step into the shoes of your employees.
Mint 15   Be there in person to celebrate long-term relationships.

Mint 16   Respect all especially those who disrespect you.
Mint 17   Respect the personal/political rights of your employees.
Mint 18   Hang proverbial mistletoe in your office.
Mint 19   Card your employees with a Hallmark Helper.
Mint 20   Infuse others to like themselves when you're around.

Part II
CONNECTION

Mint 41   Express your need for human interaction.
Mint 42   Nurture others as a Servant Leader.
Mint 43   Break out of your protective cocoon and fly high.
Mint 44   Sweeten your self-awareness with a slice of Humble Pie.
Mint 45   Leaders let others sit at the head of the table.

Mint 46   Stay true to your character no matter the distractions.
Mint 47   Play the role your audience expects.
Mint 48   Parlay the power of your patience.
Mint 49   Soften your human touch and recharge your batteries.
Mint 50   Poise under pressure enhances results.

Mint 51   Instill the thrill more than instruct the drill.
Mint 52   Be effective not just efficient in using technology.
Mint 53   Lay down a welcome mat for your office visitors.
Mint 54   Beware of turning a slap on the back into a kick in the ass.
Mint 55   Fully share responsibility and accountability.
Mint 56   Strengthen viability with creative connections.

Part III
CONVICTION

Mint 57   Stand for something or fall for anything.
Mint 58   Focus on helping others to help yourself.
Mint 59   Action is the traction to climb Mount Happiness.
Mint 60   Leaders serve others always in all ways.

Mint 61   No one is too big to fail.
Mint 62   Stay connected to your values no matter how far you wander.
Mint 63   Celebrate something bigger than you.
Mint 64   Stay in touch with the rank and file.
Mint 65   Seek an interchange of ideas with your new staff/ new hires.

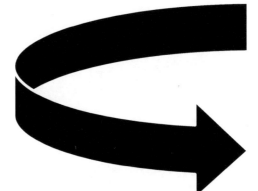

Mint 66   Someone is always watching you. You.
Mint 67   Failures: Endear 'em more than endure 'em.
Mint 68   Mistakes: new paths to continuous improvement.
Mint 69   Think ejected whenever you're rejected.
Mint 70   Press on when the pressure is on.

Mint 71   Be respectful in soothing tempers.
Mint 72   Battle back from beleaguered beginnings.
Mint 73   Change = a catalyst for continuous improvement.
Mint 74   Keep singin' in the rain no matter the strain.
Mint 75   With hope in the future, there's power in the present
Mint 76   Strive every day with all your might & no finish line in sight.
Mint 77   Competition: Catalyst for your success.

CONTENTS

Part I
COMPASSION

Part II
CONNECTION

Part II
CONVICTION

*"People will do
almost anything
if they think
they are appreciated
and if they are being
led
by someone who
cares."*

**Gerry Czarnecki, former CEO
and author of *Lead With Love***

POSTSCRIPT

To stimulate your thinking on becoming an even more effective loving leader, here's an experience the author had that informed his understanding of leading with humility and respect.

The Whale That Spouts Gets The Harpoon

Climbing over the curbed landscape barrier, the chauffeured limousine barreled over a well-manicured lawn and came to an abrupt stop in front of the corporate headquarters building – the focal point amid this lush 168-acre sculptured corporate park setting in Purchase, New York, 30 minutes north of New York City. No one else had the audacity—or the consummate authority—to chew up the grassy carpet the way that specific chauffeured limousine did most weekdays around 10 am. Don Kendall, the chairman of PepsiCo, climbed out of that limousine as if he were climbing down from a mighty stallion. He wore what appeared to be a 10-gallon cowboy hat with a commanding sense of intimidation— even if it was a classic Stetson premium quality western wear-fashion statement, reflecting his pioneering spirit that he often replenished at his get-away ranch in Pinedale, Wyoming.

With his ever-present flash and dash, it's no wonder business publications described Don Kendall in the 1970s as "burly, abrasive, ruthlessly ambitious, and forceful." Receptionists were instructed to stop whatever they were doing to acknowledge "Mr. Kendall" when he walked into the building with the bombastic flair of Don King, the hair-raising boxing promoter of that era. I never met Mr. Kendall during my 18 months at PepsiCo but I sure came away with a strong sense of what a Chief Executive Officer of a global company looked like and most importantly what it felt like to be in his (or her) presence. I was 31 then working in my first global company. Mr. Kendall was 61 and light-years away from anything I had ever known in the business world. Three weeks later I met another CEO at another global billion dollar company, Bob Pew at Steelcase Inc. in Grand Rapids, Michigan, two and half hours west of Detroit. And he also stunned me. There was the prerequisite fancy office, the specially-commissioned art, the expansive sculpture gardens, the first class corporate dining service and of course the fleet of first class airplanes. But no chauffeur. No limousine. And no 10 gallon cowboy hat. As a young executive recruit I was introduced to this chairman of the board of a multi-billion global company. He was also 61 and tall like Kendall. Both had been fighter pilots in World War II. But that's where the comparison ended.

There was no pretense.
No bombast.
No ego pounding on the chest.

Just a friendly smile and a firm handshake when I met this CEO of a very different stripe for the first time. "Bob, the name is Bob," he said with sincere eye contact. "Mr. Pew, good to meet you sir," I heard myself saying. Impulsively, I blurted back what came instinctively to my frame of reference of what it is like to be in the presence of a billion dollar global company CEO. Calmly, the patient Chairman and CEO repeated without any disdain in his voice: "The name is Bob." Stunned, I heard the words but simply could not process what he was saying and I responded instinctively like Pavlov's dogs: "Yes, Mr. Pew." He smiled again. And again in a firm but friendly tone said: "Bob."

It took me a few more seconds to process that this was a CEO from a very different business world—an alien to me. And finally I took a deep breath, realizing that all big time CEOs do not walk on water (or ride on grass). From that day on I always called him Bob just like everyone else did from the janitors to the board members. And from that day on Bob Pew taught me and everyone else he came in contact with what being a loving leader is all about. He spoke of business as a "social entity and as such it becomes a human experience." I became even more fascinated by the dichotomy of the two leaders. One proud and boastful and beaming like boxing legend Muhammad Ali telling anyone and everyone that he was "The Greatest." The other taciturn and humble, telling anyone and everyone to rein in their egotistic pride and pretense with his ever present mantra: *"The whale that spouts gets the harpoon."*

Then I became even more fascinated by how Bob Pew, a humble loving leader, built a global, industry-leader in worldwide sales during his 25 years as Chairman of Steelcase Inc, the office furniture designer and manufacturer. And then I saw in Bob Pew something I had seen in my own father: integrity. My dad showed me how a small gesture of caring rooted in integrity can build a strong partnership over time.

Cashing In
On Two Dimes

As a youngster, I remember my dad included two dimes in every greeting card he gave my mom on Valentine's Day, Mother's Day, their anniversary, her birthday etc. And every time I saw the anticipation in my mom's eyes as she cupped her left hand to catch the expected two dimes after opening the envelope. The dimes would cascade into the palm of her hand and her face would always light up in sheer delight. In gripping those dimes, she also reaffirmed her grasped on her marriage's long running experience of commitment, trust, integrity and respect that cemented their near 50-year marriage before my dad passed away. Those dimes rekindled a smoldering memory of caring and sharing, respect and understanding that to my young eyes flared the proverbial fire in their love for each other.

Anyway, this dimes-throughout-time love story began two years before my parents married. My dad was away on business serving in the United States Navy during World War II. He mailed my mom-to-be a Valentine's Day card. His testament of love for her arrived—postage due: you guessed it, 20 cents. The image of those two thin dimes over the decades seemed to carve a deeper understanding in me of what responsible caring and sharing is all about. And no doubt the symbolism reflected in those two dimes in some way played a role in my penchant to study trust-building relationships throughout most of my leadership development career. My only hope is that I have walked the talk in my own marriage to Debbie over more than 40 years. I know without her love and support and the support of our two daughters and our six grandchildren I could not have devoted the near 1,500 days it took to research and write this book.

Indeed my youngest daughter began influencing my understanding of loving leaders who care and share together when she was only a week old. My department threw a surprise baby shower for a guy, her dad. Me. This was an elaborate, well-planned event in a corporate conference room that began when I asked my boss if I could take a week of vacation when my daughter was born. He said no. I was speechless. Finally my boss said he would give me all the time off I needed but it would not count against my vacation days. "All I ask is that you be available to come in for an afternoon meeting probably towards the end of the week you're gone so that I can get your thoughts for our fiscal planning session."

After Laura was born I walked into my boss's office. He stood up and he promptly escorted me to a nearby conference room. "Surprise" chorused the group of friendly faces. I was a bit stunned more than just surprised. After all I never heard of a baby shower for a male employee. The entire department was there. There were presents, balloons and of course a spectacularly decorated huge cake with pink frosting that screamed: "Welcome Baby Laura." All I could do was smile through tears of joy and satisfaction and realize how much my boss and colleagues had paid me and my family with so much dignity and respect, so much caring and sharing, so much trust and empathy—and so much loving like a leader. Indeed work can be fun—engaging and satisfying, challenging and rewarding— if you nurture and sustain a culture that breeds loving leaders who bolster the bottom line by keeping their employees top of mind.

ACKNOWLEDGEMENTS

My thanks to the authors of the 77 plus leadership books whose insights and observation are woven throughout this book, including **James Kouzes** and **Barry Posner**. Their research on developing leaders featured in their seminal book *The Leadership Challenge* inspired both of my books in this <u>*Leadership Mints Series*</u>:

THINKING
Like a Leader
Featuring 101 Leadership Mints

&

this second book in the series:

LOVING
Like a Leader
Featuring 77 More Leadership Mints.

In addition, I especially appreciated the insights of **Gregg Cochlan** author of *Love Leadership.* His insight on love in a business context (as quoted on page 203) to drive out fear and enhance results helped me keep the theme of this book on track. I am also indebted to other authors such as Stephen R. Covey who inspired me with his mantra of "to live, to love, to learn and to leave of legacy" in his book *First Things First.* In fact without the insights of authors like Margery Williams and Rollo May, I may never have never committed myself to the four years I invested in writing and researching this book. I knew I had to confront my own feelings to write a book about feelings. And most of us (dare I be sexist and say most of us guys?) don't especially welcome talking about our feelings or baring our souls or getting all THAT real. But then I remembered what Margery Williams wrote in *The Velveteen Rabbit* about getting real:

> *"Getting real doesn't happen all at once," said the Skin Horse in The Velveteen Rabbit. "You become. It takes a long time. That's why it doesn't happen to people who break easily or have sharp edges or have to be carefully kept."*

Loving leaders don't break easily or have sharp edges or have to be carefully kept. I thank authors like Margery Williams and Rollo May for helping me develop the courage to confront my own fears and smooth out my own sharp edges in the process of writing this book. It takes courage to be vulnerable, to be humble, to bite your tongue when you feel like biting off someone's ear a la Mike Tyson.

As author Rollo May observed in his book *The Courage to Create:* "It is easier in our society to be naked physically than psychologically or spiritually, easier to share our bodies than to share our fantasies, hopes, fears and aspirations, which are felt to be more personal." That's why I especially loved the many leaders who helped me vet these *77 Leadership Mints* for their relevance and usefulness in helping busy leaders grow other leaders. In vetting these 77 Leadership Mints they kept me on track in my quest to provide leaders a tool— easy-to-use and quick-to-access—to enhance their feeling for leading. In particular many thanks to:

George Wolfe, **Ph.D**, whose insights as a former Chief Learning Officer for a global company helped me more fully connect the *77 Leadership Mints* with a three-part process of Reaching In, Reaching Down and Reaching Out. See pages 192-195. **Ken Dutkiewicz** for helping me flesh out the concept of leaders who cry for the well-being of others. **Bruce McLenithan** for walking the talk as a loving leader whose caring and sharing persona inspired and challenged me. **Mike Wykes** for his keen editing eye and insight on leadership behaviors. **Dave Lathrop** for his insight on the importance of storytelling to enhance understanding. **Craig Smith** for his insights in defining and aligning behavioral talent. And **Tim Penning, Ph.D**, for his insights on research.

Now I look forward to learning from you—the reader—on your experience as a loving leader or as an engaged follower of a loving leader. How does your experience resonate with the following insight (first discussed on page 204)? Gerry Czarnecki, the former CEO and author of *Lead With Love* says:

"People will do almost anything
if they think
they are appreciated
and if they are being led
by someone who cares."

Validate or refute that observation. Write us a letter sharing your experiences as a loving leader or as a follower of a loving leader. Your letter could be published in a future edition of **LOVING Like a Leader**.

Consider the example of a Letter to a Loving Leader beginning on the next page. It's a letter from a follower whose shared personal experience helps us all come to a better understanding of the influential role of a loving leader. See how easily a leader can inadvertently smother the flame of a newly lit employee's creative fire or how deliberately a loving leader can fan the flame with dignity and respect that kindles greater productivity and profitability. Perhaps the following letter will trigger your own thoughts on becoming an even more committed loving leader or loyal follower.

Dear Loving Leader:

I've been thinking a lot, lately, about our time together – the good and the bad – and today I felt like writing you a letter. No, not a letter of resignation. Rather, a letter of thanks. For all you have done for me, I want to say "Way to go!" You probably don't hear it all that often, but you've made a huge impact on me both as a person and as a professional. It all started on the very first day I came to work. How? Simple. You made me feel welcome.

When I showed up, my work space was prepared and my supplies were laid out, ready for me to use. There was even a little note card from you that said, "Welcome." And my favorite thing of all? You left a fancy mug with the company's logo on my desk. So cool. I know what you're probably thinking – that's silly, that's basic stuff. But, you'd be surprised. I had a boss at another company who didn't say hello to me on my first day. She went as far as to pass me in the hallway without even a glance. I remember it well:

As I saw her approach from the other end of a long hallway, I straightened my back, cracked my best smile and readied my hand for a firm handshake, to be followed by a pleasant "good morning." But, nothing. She passed me and kept going. I never forgot that.

So, please know what a huge impact you had on me that day you were ready for my arrival. I know you are incredibly busy, and it made me feel special and loyal to this company from the very start. I could stop there, but that's not all I want to give thanks for today. There was another time when you pulled me into your office to tell me I wasn't meeting your expectations. Do you remember that? I remember, because you did it with such finesse and grace. I could have left that meeting feeling like a lesser person, but you made the exact opposite happen! Instead, while I did leave your office feeling sad about how I had disappointed you, more importantly, I felt optimistic that I knew how to do better and could improve.

One thing you said to me really stood out: "If you want to get to the next level, perform like you're already there." A short time after that meeting, you caught me doing the very thing that you asked me to do, and you stopped me in the hall to tell me that I had nailed it. You said: "That was perfect. Do more of that!" So, I did.

Those were the early days of our time together when I was green and needed your close guidance. But, somewhere along the way, things changed. For the better. Like, just last year when you called a meeting with me to talk about your strategic five-year goals. I remember thinking, "This is very interesting, but why is she telling me all this?" But, by the time you were done, it was all clear. To my surprise, you were asking me to take the lead on one of your new initiatives. Yes, I was excited, but there was only one BIG problem. I had absolutely no idea how to do the thing you were asking of me.

But, that didn't seem to bother you. Not one bit. To me, you said: "No worries. I trust that you can do this. And, I'll help. "So we did it. And it was great. I feel like I'm gushing, but I can't end this letter without also acknowledging how well you've supported me personally during some of the hardest times. Like, when I had a sick family member in the hospital. You didn't make me feel bad for something I couldn't control or guilty for not being at work. Instead, you said: "Go, take care of your family. We'll handle things until you get back." I'll never forget how that made me feel and how much you helped me and my family.

I hope you see that, from my perspective, things have been going well with us. You're a great leader, and I never want that to change. You asked me once to never hold back on giving YOU feedback. So, while I have your attention, I'll just take this opportunity to share how I want you to continue to lead me. Here are a few tips on the best ways to lead me:

- **Continue trusting** and pushing me, and giving me space to do my best work.
- **Start spending more time** with me. Your attention is invaluable for my development.
- **Stop taking on too much work** yourself. Use me. I'm up for the challenge!

In closing, one more time, I want to sincerely say *thank you* for all that you've done and will do for me. It is because of you that I continue to work for this company and enjoy what I get to do every day. I look forward to what's to come, whatever that may be.

From Your Follower,

Alan

Alan Derek Utley
San Antonio, Texas

Insights at-a-Glance

To stimulate your own feelings and thoughts on becoming an even more effective loving leader, here are a few excerpts and the Mint # source.

- Mutual trust is sown not sewn: grown day in and day out over time not something stitched together in time. *(Mint 27)*

- Loving leaders know that no machines, no robotics, no technology can operate without a MANual. *(Mint 52)*

- The tears of a loving leader are shed for what is significant to others—what's pithy—not what's a pity. *(Mint 3)*

- Trust like empathy is something you do, not something you have. Trust like empathy is something you give not something you demand. *(Mint 26)*

- Loving leaders listen first where the other is coming from more than simply where they're from. *(Mint 25)*

- When feelings more than facts are shared, trust soars and mutual understanding and confidence ensues. **(Mint 21)**

- Pollinating the blossoming of others like a bee is an instructive metaphor to bee or not to bee a loving leader. **(Mint 24)**

- Loving leaders become more self-less and less selfish. They say " I am sorry" and "Thank you" often. **(Mint 25)**

More Insights at-a-Glance

- Loving leaders are willing to stand in public wearing only their BVDs: Beliefs, Values and Disciplines. *(Mint 57)*

- Loving leaders cope with hope. *(Mint 75*)

- Trust is given based on a loving leader's expectation of another rather than trust earned by the leader's inspection of another. *(Mint 27)*

- Loving leaders and their employees work with each other not for one another. They need each other to bring out the best in each other the way every bell needs clapper or every bow needs an arrow. *(Mint 6)*

- Loving leaders can step away from their own ego and arrogance long enough to bathe in the glow of another's ideas, notions and opinions. *(Mint 7)*

- You lead best when your feelings are thoughtfully released not simply emotionally unleashed— when your feelings are freed from confinement or restraint not simply set loose to pursue. *(Mint 2)*

- Think of your mistakes as a "miss-take." A "take" in the movies is the uninterrupted filming of a scene. A "miss" is something off target. So a miss-take —or a mistake—is an off-target scene. *(Mint 68)*

Q&A

Here's an excerpt of an interview
with the author Peter Jeff on the creative intent
and value-added significance of
LOVING Like a Leader,
Featuring 77 More Leadership Mints:

What's the Unique Selling Point of this book?

Leadership development on-the-go. You don't have to sit down to read this book for 15-30 minutes or more at a time as if it were a meal. You can digest this book one bite at a time in 5 minutes or less as if it were a candy mint: easily accessed, quickly digested and immediately refreshing. That's why this book is structured around <u>Leadership Mints</u> not chapters.

What's a Leadership Mint?

A Leadership Mint is a short story that personalizes leadership development principles with examples from business, sports and politics. In addition, those stories cite insights from more than 77 other leadership books, making **LOVING Like a Leader** a quick-read, leadership development reference book that combines the story-telling of an inspirational book like *Chicken Soup for the Soul* by Jack Canfield and Mark Victor Hansen with the documentation, case studies and research of *The Leadership Challenge,* the most–sold leadership development book in the world (1.5 million copies) by James Kouzes and Barry Posner.

What's a Leadership Mints Break?

A Leadership Mints Break is a 5-minute leadership development learning opportunity that can help a leader quickly share a Leadership Mint with his or her team during their regular staff meetings. To more fully focus on the intended message in that Mint, each short story begins with the key take-away called Today's EngageMINT, a one-sentence summary intended to engage the reader in that particular leadership behavior.

More Q&A

What's new and different about the content?

Edutainment. The content is designed to entertain as much as educate. Consider the desk of a CEO that is decorated with six yo-yos *(Mint 62)* or a nine foot tall photograph of a Sequoia Tree *(Mint 61)* featuring a CEO's office or the CEO who installs a "snotline" in his office *(Mint 37)*. The entertaining value of the book includes a 10 page section on tips and techniques to hone your sense of humor as a loving leader. In addition, if you're having a bad day getting started on a new project, take solace in Mint 72 (hey at least you weren't born dead, see page 175). And if you're frustrated over failing or making mistakes, take respite in Mint 67 and Mint 68 (pages 161-166).

What is the bottom-line significance of the book?

Productivity in real time. This book is filled with ideas on conflict management, negotiation, and coaching that are always at the finger-tips of a leader – much like a candy mint dish – to grab and go when a leader's intervention can do the most good in real time. Too often we send emerging and seasoned leaders to webinars, workshops and seminars and fill them up with information and tools that somehow never get dusted off in the real world. Think of this book as a bowl of 77 mints to refresh a loving leader's compassion, connection and conviction.

What is the intent of this book?

The intent of this book on leadership development is to become the most re-read book on leadership development: a key reference tool in real time for all leaders to preserve, protect and promote their feeling for leading.

How can I find specific ways to become a loving leader?

Turn to the Afterword (page 211) for specific initiatives on how to become an effective loving leader. Turn to the Epilogue (page 199) to assess the business rationale for loving like a leader. And turn to page 237 to see a list of all 77 EngageMINTS, the one-line key learning summary that leads each Leadership Mint.

June 3, 1963

Dear Jay:

Happy Birthday! Just a note to tell you how much you have meant to me personally. Over the past 25+ years we have had our differences, but something greater has always shown through.

I don't know if there is any simple way to say it, but it could be called mutual respect. A better word could be love.

Sincerely,

Rich

Rich DeVos sent the above note to Jay Van Andel on his 39th birthday. The high school pals became life-long business partners, billionaires and philanthropic leaders. They partnered in 1959 to found the Amway Corporation that grew into a $7 billion worldwide consumer products company and inspired thousands of other entrepreneurs who became millionaires after enlisting in the American Way business plan (a.k.a. Amway). Their secret to success: love. See page 204. "Many partnerships are weakened by selfishness, greed and disloyalty," wrote Rich DeVos in the foreword of Jay Van Andel's 1998 biography *An Enterprising Life,* "but Jay and I built our relationship on mutual respect and caring."

Further Reading
77-plus books referenced in *LOVING Like a Leader*

Argument Culture, Deborah Tannen
Art of Winning, Dennis Conner
Arts of Man, Eric Newton
As a Man Thinketh, James Allen
Authentic Leadership, Bill George

Certain Trumpets, Garry Wills
Charisma Myth, Olivia Fox Cabane
Contented Cows Still Give Better Milk, , Bill Catlette, Richard Hadden
Corner Office, Adam Bryant
Democracy in America, Alexis de Tocqueville
Disney Way, Bill Capodagli, Lynn Jackson
Dynamics of Self-Fulfillment, Dr. Arnold Hutschnecker

Emotional Intelligence, Daniel Goleman
Everybody Matters, Bob Chapman, Raj Sisodia
Executive Warfare, David D'Alessandro
Eye Witness to Power, David Gergen

Fierce Conversations, Susan Scott
Five Languages of Love, Gary Chapman
For Whom the Bell Tolls, Ernest Hemingway
Friendship Factor, Alan Loy McGinnis

Good Boss, Bad Boss, Robert Sutton
Good to Great, James Collins
Grapes of Wrath, John Steinbeck

Harry S. Truman, David McCullough
Higher Standard of Leadership, Keshauan Nair
Hope Is Not a Method, General Gordon Sullivan
How to Win Friends and Influence People, Dale Carnegie
Human Connections, John R. Diekman

In the Arena, Richard Nixon
It Worked For Me, General Colin Powell
It's Your Ship, Capt. D. Michael Abrashoff

John Adams, David McCullough
Lead With Love, Gerry Czarnecki
Lead With LUV, Ken Blanchard, Colleen Barrett
Leader in Me, Stephen R. Covey
Leader in You, Stuart R. Levine, Michael A. Crom
Leader Within, Howard Haas
Leadership Challenge, James Kouzes, Barry Posner
Leadership Is An Art, Max De Pree

Leadership Jazz, Max De Pree
Leadership On The Line, Ron Heifetz, Marty Linsky
Leadership, James MacGregor Burns

Leadership: A Very Short Introduction, Keith Grint
Lead from the Heart, Mark Crowley
Leading Without Power, Max De Pree
Learn to Lead With Love, Robert Siegel, Jr
Life Craft, Reverend Forrest Church
Long Walk to Freedom, Nelson Mandela

LOVE 2.0, Barbara Fredrickson
Love and Profit, James Autry
Love Leadership, Gregg Cochlan
Love Works, Joel Manby
Loving Each Other, Leo Buscaglia

Made in America, Sam Walton
Man's Search for Meaning, Viktor Frankl
Managing as a Performing Art, Peter Vaill
Mask of Command, John Keegan
Millionaire Mind, Thomas J. Stanley
Motivation & Personality, Abraham Maslow
New One Minute Manager, Ken Blanchard, Spencer Johnson
Opera 101, Fred Plitkin

Peace of Mind, Joshua Liebman
Peak Performance, Jon Katzenbach
Prince of Tides, Pat Conroy
Quick and Nimble, Adam Bryant
Real Power, James Autry, Stephen Mitchell
Rise of Teddy Roosevelt, Edmund Morris
Road to Character, David Brooks
Silicon Snake Oil, Clifford Stoll
Servant Leadership, Robert K. Greenleaf
Summoned to Lead, Leonard Sweet
THINKING Like a Leader, Peter Jeff
Ultimate Competitive Advantage, Shawn Moon, Sue Daeth-Douglass
Undaunted Courage, Stephen Ambrose

Way We're Working Isn't Working, Tony Schwartz
West Point Leadership Lessons, Scott Snair
Who Moved My Cheese, Spencer Johnson
When Pride Still Mattered, David Maraniss
Why Work, Mike Maccoby
Winning From Within, Erica Ariel Fox
Work Spirit, Sharon Louise Connelly
World's Most Powerful Leadership Principle, James Hunter
You're in Charge, Now What? Thomas Neff, James M. Citrin
Zadig, Voltaire

5 Dysfunctions of a Team, Patrick Lencioni
12 Disciplines of Leadership Excellence, Brian Tracey, Dr. Peter Chee
12 Lessons from the Life of Jesus Christ, Kimball Fisher
21 Irrefutable Laws of Leadership, John Maxwell
33 Unwritten Rules of Management, Bill Swanson

INDEX

A

COVER DESIGN

The basic black color scheme establishes the disciplined bottom-line business tone and even more significantly the bold white type on a black background showcases the underlying theme of the book: we need each other to bring out the best in each other.

THINKING
Like a Leader

The first book in the <u>Leadership Mints Series</u> is titled: *THINKING Like a Leader, Featuring 101 Leadership Mints.* Here's an excerpt from Mint 34.

The most thoughtful leaders and engaged employees know their lives are more effectively connected NOT on-line but IN LINE —in person— IN LINE with others at your grocery store, deli, coffee house etc. There IN LINE–face-to-face–you don't need a mouse or keyboard to click with a friend. All you need is a smile and a common interest stirred with an openness to learn from, to share with, and to listen to. Yet the flurry of bits and bytes invading 24/7 from cyberspace keep gnawing away at the potential of a leader. That's why a former Yale University leadership development professor in a guest lecture to plebes at West Point Academy challenged the 19-year-old freshmen to invest themselves personally in more face-to-face, no-screen required relationships rather than "have 968 'friends' that we never actually talk to," William Deresiewicz said.

Yet, too many leaders say they are too busy to seek the solitude that Deresiewicz says is "the essence of leadership." But how many would-be leaders are just too busy being busy: too busy thumbing their way merrily along the cyber highway and too busy paying homage to the Texting and Tweeting gods to be a friend to SomeONE let alone find a friend with anyone? How do you take the time to make a friend and dedicate the time to be a friend? First make a friend of yourself. Turn off your devices and turn on to yourself. Be silent and listen to yourself. Consider those two words <u>Listen</u> and <u>Silent</u>. Scramble the letters and one becomes the other: silent and listen have the same letters in different order as author John Canfield notes. How can you most effectively be silent and listen to yourself? First get comfortable in your own skin. And then be willing to let SOMEONE get under your skin to stimulate your feeling, to inspire your thinking and to energize your leading.

About the Author

Peter Jeff is a leadership development consultant and coach. He held a ringside seat in the C-Suite of a multi-billion dollar global industrial leader for more than 25 years where he consulted with executive management on a range of leadership issues from conflict management to employee engagement.

Contact: E-mail: peterjeff@charter.net
Tweet: @LeaderMintsGuy
Visit: www.LeadershipMints.com

LOVING Like a Leader
Featuring
77 More Leadership Mints

Please send your letters to loving leaders for possible publication in a future edition of *LOVING Like a Leader.*
(See example page 252.)